"I Just Want To Be Loved!"

"I Just Want To Be Loved!"

The Journey from Your Head *Back* to Your Heart

SUSAN FAYE DAVIS

BALBOA.
PRESS

A DIVISION OF HAY HOUSE

Balboa Press books may be ordered through booksellers or by contacting:

Balboa Press
A Division of Hay House
1663 Liberty Drive
Bloomington, IN 47403
www.balboapress.com
1-(877) 407-4847

Because of the dynamic nature of the Internet, any web addresses or
links contained in this book may have changed since publication and
may no longer be valid. The views expressed in this work are solely those
of the author and do not necessarily reflect the views of the publisher,
and the publisher hereby disclaims any responsibility for them.

The author of this book does not dispense medical advice or prescribe the use
of any technique as a form of treatment for physical, emotional, or medical
problems without the advice of a physician, either directly or indirectly. The
intent of the author is only to offer information of a general nature to help you
in your quest for emotional and spiritual well-being. In the event you use any
of the information in this book for yourself, which is your constitutional right,
the author and the publisher assume no responsibility for your actions.

Cover image provided by Thinkstock,
and such images are being used for illustrative purposes only.
Certain stock imagery © Thinkstock.

Printed in the United States of America.

ISBN: 978-1-4525-7990-0 (sc)
ISBN: 978-1-4525-7991-7 (e)

Library of Congress Control Number: 2013914712

Balboa Press rev. date: 08/27/2013

Please Note, Very Important:

Dedication

To all of us willing to face our fears
In search of a more fulfilling life.

A Message from Spirit

"I am here for you even when
you are not aware of me."
My Spirit Speaks, but Do I Choose to Listen?
"I Am Peace, Calm, Love and Joy,
Reflecting the Beauty of You."
"I Am Your True Essence, All You Seek."
"Stop Searching and Listen."
"Close Your Eyes. Can You Feel Me?"

"I am here for you even when
you are not aware of me."
"Will You Join Me? I Am You,
There is Nothing to Fear."
"What I Am, is What You Long to Be."

"I am here for you even when
you are not aware of me."

by Susan Faye Davis

Table of Contents

Preface

My passion is to share the message and raise awareness that self love is the one principle that will transform our lives into all we desire. My personal emotional baggage was unsuccessful weight management, constantly beating myself up for over 30 years, losing the unhealthy weight only to gain back even more, my fears buried in low self esteem. Another strong influence was my brother's personal battle to overcome his lack of self love, a battle which he lost.

About 13 years ago I began my path back to reconnecting with my true Spirit, this process is challenging, educational, emotional, and fulfilling. As I continue to stretch into new, uncomfortable territories, I continually wonder if my discomfort is due to unfamiliar territory, or am I uncomfortable addressing issues that need to be healed and dissolved.

"I Just Want To Be Loved!" The Journey from Your Head Back to Your Heart, was actually born as an 'Aha' moment about 7 years ago. Having arrived at a place in my life where I decided that there was a tragic amount of unnecessary emotional suffering in our world. I felt my Spirit calling me to somehow raise the awareness that we have the ability to overcome our limiting perceptions and beliefs. We have the power to change our thoughts and behaviors to create the lives we desire, lives overflowing with happiness, love, purpose, and fulfillment.

As a result of this journey my credentials now include nutritional consultant, master herbalist, holistic health practitioner, and certified medical support clinical hypnotherapist. In creating the written materials for both my private practice and various workshops "I Just Want To Be Loved!" evolved. The opposite of fear is love. Self Love is the one answer, the one principle that leads us back to our Spirit to reconnect with our source, to live the abundance that is naturally ours.

Introduction

We cannot truly love or be loved by another until first we love ourselves. Giving and receiving love begins with self love. The purpose of our existence is to love ourselves unconditionally so that we may love each other unconditionally.

Living from a place of love, living from our heart, connected to our Spirit, connected to our Source, only then are we able to express love in our actions and interactions connecting with each other. When we live from love we experience happiness, abundance, joy, prosperity, and fulfillment. Living from a place of love is living a life of bliss, living Heaven on Earth, living as we were designed to live, living our divine purpose.

Without love there is fear.

The opposite of love is fear.

When we move away from love we become disconnected from our heart. Moving away from love, away from our heart away from our spirit, we move into living in fear, living in our head, directed by our mind we live in ego and fear.

Living in fear is separation, disconnected from our Spirit, our Source, and each other. When we live from a place of fear we experience lack, anger, judgment, unhappiness, and loneliness.

When our life is no longer working for us, we are receiving a message from our Spirit that it is time to take a journey moving from our head back to our heart, move out of fear and back into love. Living from a place of love begins with Self Love. *Self love is to love and accept ourselves, completely and unconditionally.* We must first love ourselves before it is possible to truly, unconditionally love others.

Congratulations for having the courage to listen to and act on the message from your Spirit, signaling that a change is necessary to attract what you desire into your life. *Please trust that you are not broken, you are not alone and you do not need to be fixed, you are in the right place, at exactly the right time in your life.* You have not missed out, it is not too late. Today, as you begin to read, relax, know that all is in perfect order, all is in Divine Order. Right now in this moment you are the sum total of all your life experiences. Be present *now*, set aside the past experiences that you cannot change and set aside the worries of the future that have not happened. You are embarking on a new path, a path that will guide you in experiencing a richer, happier, more fulfilling life, a life of purpose. The first step in creating the life you desire begins with loving yourself. To love your self is total self acceptance, taking responsibility for your thoughts, responsibility for your feelings and actions, being compassionate and forgiving with yourself, being your own best friend, no matter what or who happens in your life. Now, with mindfulness let us begin together this exciting journey of rediscovery. *'I just want to be loved'* will be your guide on the journey from your head where fear and ego live, back to your heart, the home of your Spirit, to live in self love, to live from a place of love.

This guide was designed in two phases, Phase I, explains the what, why and how of the situation we find ourselves in today, our current reality. Phase II, demonstrates the actions necessary to create our new reality and how to maintain it.

Phase I reviews what self love is and why it is so fundamental to our happiness and fulfillment. We examine why we awaken one day and find ourselves asking "Whose life is this?" We uncover why we wake up one day very unhappy, ill or we find ourselves in the middle of a life changing event. We then discuss how we gradually move from our original connection to Spirit, God, Source during our formative years to the present day disconnect. As you read through these chapters you will be guided in reconnecting with your Spirit, God, Source. We discuss the process of taking responsibility for the lives we created, our current reality, and the importance of developing our self awareness. We demonstrate the value of connecting with our emotions and the journey of returning to a place of love by acknowledging our fears. This is the process of moving from your head *back* to your heart, where your true Spirit lives, where you live from a place of love, peace, calm, knowing and fulfillment. When you return home to live life from your heart again, you reconnect with your Spirit, which lives in your heart even when you are not aware of it.

Phase II contains daily practice exercises and methods that will support you in achieving successful positive change and in developing a stronger connection to your Spirit, to God, Source, to the Universe. Some of these methods may be familiar; others may be new to you. Please consider the daily practices an exploration process, experience each of the different practices at least once or twice, then decide what method(s) are the most comfortable and rewarding experiences for you. Keeping an open and willing mind creates an element of anticipation. As you begin to awaken your Spirit you may rediscover buried talents and reignite your creativity though your imagination, visualizing your desires fulfilled. Experience the power of journaling exercises with both your spirit, for guidance, and your inner child, to re-connect with play, a vital element for a balanced life. Learn how to develop daily Gratitude, Self Love and Appreciation to raise your energy vibration, attracting more of the good you desire into your life. Deepen your connection to Self, Spirit, God, Source with the daily practice of affirmations, prayer, meditation, and self hypnosis. Finally to assist in your continuing journey of self discovery and fulfillment, an additional suggested reading list has been included in the last pages.

It is natural for us to live from our hearts in self love, a returning home, to be guided by our Spirit, living in harmony and balance with the power of our mind and the strength of our body!

Living Your Spirit = Self Love

Living From Your Heart = Living From a Place of Love

Phase I

The What, Why & How Of
Your Current Reality

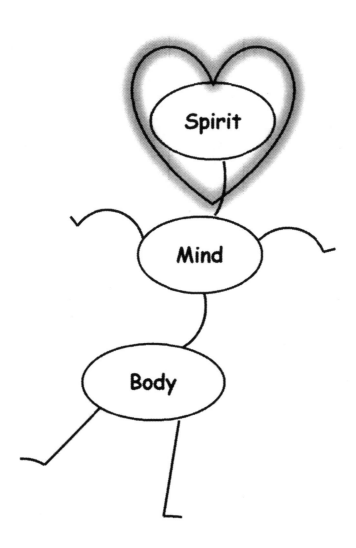

Chapter 1

"I just want to be loved!"
What is love?

If we examine this statement for a moment, the word *Love is a feeling, an emotion.* The question we ask, "*Is the need to be loved the exclusive emotion that controls our entire human experience?*"

What makes us happy?

We are happy when we *Feel:*

Appreciated   Acknowledged   Needed

Valued   Connected   Worthy   Desired   Accepted

All of these words describe the *Emotions* we

Feel* when we are *Loved.

Why is love fundamental to our happiness?

Love and Spirit both live in our hearts, our Spirit is love, our purpose is to love and be loved, it is our nature to be happy.

When we are not living in our hearts from a place of love, we are living from a place of fear, we are living in our heads, when living in fear we are unhappy.

How do we fulfill our desire to be loved?

For us to feel loved we must first love ourselves unconditionally, this is self love, only then will we have the ability to give and receive love.

Before we begin our journey from our head, where we live in fear and disconnect, *back* to a place of love, living from our heart connected to our Spirit and our Source, there are two concepts to accept. *The first concept is we must love ourselves before we will experience a fulfilling and abundant life, and the second concept is what we are searching for is only found inside of us. Persons and things outside of ourselves may enrich our lives, but they only provide temporary love and happiness.*

As defined earlier self love is the total acceptance of *'you'*. Consciously we may believe we love ourselves, that we make the best choices to support our desired success. However sub-consciously, or unconsciously, we may have another belief, for example a belief that we are not worthy of our desired success. Using this example, the belief of being unworthy is what really drives the choices we make; this limiting belief is what sabotages our success. As we take the journey through the first few chapters we will discover why we disconnect and how these limiting beliefs are formed. We will learn the steps necessary to change our reality by developing greater awareness and acknowledging our emotions, eliminating un-necessary fears so that we can live from our hearts, from a place of love and ultimately achieve the fulfilling life we desire. This is the process of re-discovering self love, the journey from your head back to you heart.

The second concept we will examine first, the idea that although persons and things may enrich our lives, no person or thing outside of ourselves will fulfill or love us completely or permanently because what we search for is only found inside of us, love, peace, fulfillment, happiness begin from the inside. *"What you seek is already inside of you"* means that love, happiness, fulfillment is found inside of you, your connection to yourself, your connection to Spirit, to God, to Source. This second concept is a fundamental point that we will address now. At this juncture I ask that for now you accept the concept, 'what you seek is already inside of you', as being true. I am confident that you will agree with this statement after you have completed your reading and experienced the daily practices.

In the journey from our head back to our heart we learn that we must stop looking to others to love us in order to feel complete, happy or fulfilled. Looking outside of ourselves before we accept and love ourselves will never fill the void of happiness and fulfillment. How can we ask someone else to do for us what we are not willing to do for ourselves? How can we ask someone else to love us, accept us just the way we are when we do not see ourselves as worthy of love or success?

The root of all human suffering

Is the lack of self love

And our inability to receive

The love we desire from others.

Consider if you will, this question, "What happens when the need to be loved, acknowledged and appreciated is not fulfilled?" *When we ask for or desire to receive the feeling of love, acknowledgement, or appreciation from another, we are asking for a feeling to be given to us so that we can feel better about ourselves.* If the person does not give us the love, acknowledgement or appreciation in the *'manner'* that we desire according to our perception, we feel sad, unhappy, unworthy, unloved. When we seek positive feelings from outside of ourselves and are unsuccessful at obtaining those feelings, we are left feeling unfulfilled, we feel frustration, loneliness, stress, the misery of not feeling worthy, or the feeling of being disconnected from others, feeling out of place, feeling that we do not fit in.

My brother was a motivating force behind my passion to study the relationship between the lack of self love and the resulting levels of self inflicted pain it creates. My brother, Jimmy, was lost to me and his loved ones at a young age due to what I recognize now as a lack of self love. His inability to love himself first prevented him from receiving the love that was abundantly available to him, given freely and willingly to him by his loved ones. Jimmy was always restless, as if searching for something, but without knowing what he was searching for. He tried adventure to fill the void, finding that unsatisfying, he experimented with behaviors outside of what mainstream deemed acceptable in attempts to attract love, attention and approval. When his behavior received attention, he decided his personal truth, "any type of attention, positive or negative, was the sign of love he was searching for". He based his truth on the observation that "if you are paying attention to me, you must care, therefore you love me". His behavior demonstrated that he never felt he received the love he was searching for. His loved ones were certainly providing love to him in the best way they knew how; they loved him, however not in the manner in which he was searching for. Jimmy was unaware that his lack of self love is what blocked him from receiving the love he desired from others. Only by loving himself first, would he be open to receive the love from others. *Seeking approval, acceptance, acknowledgement, connection, love, from others to make us happy, is a limiting belief that leads to a lifetime of disappointment, depression and desperation.*

When we seek outside of ourselves for fulfillment, for total acceptance, for complete and perfect love, we will be disappointed 100% of the time. What we seek is found inside of us. We are responsible for our own happiness, fulfillment and self love. Yes, others enrich our lives, adding so much more to what we have and already are. Yes, we desire fulfilling relationships and love from our partners, family members and community. When you are loved and appreciated by others, life is even better, you wear rose color glasses, say 'hello' to strangers, your perception is that everyone is well intentioned towards you, you are calm, happy, all is right with the world and if it is not, that is okay, you only see the positive. You feel good, you feel loved, so you forgive or overlook negative actions, it is like being in a loving relationship for the first time, all is right with the world. When you have a positive outlook, you create a higher vibration; this higher vibration attracts more good into your life! Life is good; it just gets better and better! Life just gets better when we are loved by others.

The caution here is that seeking love, acknowledgement, and appreciation from outside sources to make us feel better is only *temporary* because change is always a constant especially when relying on outside influences. The only way to create permanent love is to create your own self love by turning within, by re-connecting to your Spirit, to God, to Source. When you strengthen your connection you become comfortable with yourself, you are able to choose your emotions, create a peaceful reality of love and appreciation of yourself, this then allows you to see and accept others as they are, opening up the unlimited possibilities of quality relationships. We must begin with ourselves first before we can truly love and accept others as they are. Your higher energy vibration will attract all of the right people into your life. This higher energy will affect all aspects of your life, family, career, and personal relationships.

No external source, person or possessions can make you happy, feel loved or feel fulfilled, the feelings are only temporary, subject to another persons' whim to withhold love or influence your emotions with their bad mood or unkind words. Consider for a moment the stress we put on ourselves by relying on the economy, low interest rates, unpredictable real estate market, stock profits and losses to make us happy? How lasting is happiness in purchasing the newest technology, jewelry or car, the latest trendy material possession? The good feelings fading as the novelty wears off. Love, satisfaction, happiness, fulfillment and accomplishment are temporary feelings when found outside of ourselves. This is not to say that money and material possessions are not fantastic rewards and gifts in life! Shopping is fun, playing with expensive toys are exciting. We just need to create our solid foundation first. Real love, joy, happiness, satisfaction are found on the inside. Once we develop awareness we choose our feelings, we create our reality, and we decide how we react to external situations.

Over the next few chapters we will take the journey from our head, where we live from a place of fear, disconnected, alone, unhappy and perhaps in dis-ease, back to our heart, where we were originally connected to our Spirit, our Source, God, or the Universe. All you seek is already inside of you; we are just changing our limiting thoughts that no longer serve our purpose. It is not by accident that you are reading this book right now at this point in your life. You are in the right place at the right time, Divine Order is at work. You are ready to re-connect with that small voice inside of you that is sending you the messages that it is time for a change. The small voice inside of you, your Spirit, your intuition, your inner child, your higher wisdom, the part of you that longs to be happy, to enjoy life again, is sending you a message that something in your life is no longer working and it is time to make a change.

Back to the first concept, we need to love ourselves before we will experience a fulfilling and abundant life. 'Only you have what you need' is not a statement referring to a life of solitude, 'you against the world' or 'that you are alone, an army of one' but rather the opposite, when you look inside and love yourself first, you are in the world connected to your Spirit, connected to God, to Source, to others. When you are living from self love, living from your heart, you are connected to your Spirit you are enjoying all the possibilities available to you, living the perfect true expression of yourself! Life is easy and flowing. You live a life of anticipation for the next good thing coming into your life you attract exactly what you need when you need it into your life. Happy, joyful, each day filled with possibilities! Sound wonderful, sound too good to be true? It is true; it is this simple, but not necessarily easy. To return to your heart and rediscover self love takes a commitment from you to follow the daily practices, change your negative thoughts, change old patterns and develop more positive self empowering behaviors and beliefs.

When you choose the path of developing greater self love, you open yourself up to all the glorious possibilities of life. Abundance in *all* aspects of your life is available to you, more fulfilling relationships with your partner, family and friends, more financial prosperity providing monetary and material possessions, greater professional success and deeper spiritual living with purpose and fulfillment. Living from a place of true self love is living the perfect self expression of yourself, all of your desires to experience your highest good are realized, even better than you could ever imagine!

In self love we enjoy who we are, we appreciate what we are, and we go through the day in a positive loving way, looking at each situation with love. When we love ourselves, we open to all of the beauty that is in us and around us. Love is the opposite of fear. Self love removes all pain, worry, doubt, fear, and hate. Love is living from your heart; fear is living from your head.

We are divine spiritual beings here for a human experience. We are connected to the Universe, to each other, to a higher Source. There is beauty, abundance, love, and peace, unlimited possibilities all ready inside of us, just waiting to be expressed and experienced. All we have to do is open ourselves up to receive. When we are ready to receive we are ready to give, participating in the constant flow of abundance. All we need is inside of us, we just need to turn inside and connect with our Spirit.

The journey from our heads back to our hearts is based on the belief that when we first address the lack of self love and change our limiting beliefs, we 'recreate' our lives based in self love, each of us taking responsibility for our lives. Once we accept knowing that self love comes from 'inside', not something outside of ourselves, we begin the path back to living our Spirit. Once we remember and accept that we have the ability to create our own joy, peace, and a purposeful life, we are able to raise our energy level and attract more of the good we desire into our lives. From a place of love we will remember, or re-discover, that we are connected to Source, God, Spirit, Universe, Mother Earth, and to each other. In self love we then feel connected, supported, appreciated, and loved by others creating the peace, calm, and joy we seek. By living in self love we are able to live our passions with purpose because we are no longer afraid, fear is replaced by love.

I believe each one of us, are Spiritual beings that have chosen to have a human experience and we are living in heaven here on earth. I believe that as we evolve to higher levels of peace, joy and fulfillment, living our Spirit in self love, we live our chosen life with purpose, the life we were destine to create before we disconnected from our Spirit, Source, Higher Selves. This higher energy vibration connects us with those around us, and expands to connect all beings on the entire planet. Ah, living from the heart in love, living heaven on earth is a much happier perception of life!

I would like to provide definitions to clarify a few words chosen for the purposes of this guide for two reasons. First, it is my sincere desire for you to continue reading as I feel passionately about guiding as many of us as possible out of unnecessary pain and/or self imposed suffering due to lack of self love. Second, the complexities of words and language are so vast they require specific definitions. It is important to note that each of us has a different perception, so words have a different meaning to each of us. My interpretation of a word is based on my *'personal perception'*, which is filtered through my personal history, limiting belief, or the lie I decided about myself at a young age, or during a trauma/drama event. Your interpretation of a word is based on your 'personal perception', your filter. You draw your meaning of the word and what it means to you based on what you decided about yourself. We are aware that words hold different interpretation depending on what part of the country, or what country we are in. For example in the United States, some areas use the word 'soda' whereas other areas use the word 'pop', and some use the word 'sack' to refer to a 'bag'. Examples between English speaking countries would be 'water closet' versus 'restroom' and 'lift' versus 'elevator'. *"Think of our personal perception as our own unique language."* When we communicate with others we each hear the words as familiar, believing we know what the other means as we each filter our words through our own personal perception language. In successful communication we need to remember each of us believe we know what the other means and that we believe we are expressing ourselves clearly. In reality both parties are unaware of the exact meaning of the words each is hearing from the other. As a side note, remaining open and listening is always helpful in effective communications.

Another aspect of 'personal perception' and the complexities of effective communication is the acceptable degree of public expression of phrases or statements. For example, some may easily say 'I Love you' many times a day to those dear to them. Others may have difficulty speaking the words 'I Love you' even once during a day to a dear family member. Does one love the other less because they do not speak the feelings out loud or as often? Personal perception is what is true for you.

Definitions

Self Love is to love yourself as the beautiful perfect spirit that you are, to love and appreciate your human form, to appreciate all that you are, to be your own best friend. What self love is not, "I take care of me first at the harm of others. I am the only one who matters. I am more important or better than anyone else".

Create our own Reality, create our own life, means you choose the life you want to live as a result of your thoughts and actions.

Take Responsibility for your life is to accept that you created your life and only you can change it, you are not a victim, and you do not blame others for your choices.

Remember / Re discover that we are connected to Spirit, Source, God, Universe and our calling, our purpose, is still inside of us, it has just been buried over the years.

Connected means we are all one energetically, connected to our Spirit, Source, God, Universe

Disconnect is to move from heart to head in fear and ego, you decided the personal lie or limiting beliefs about you, moving away from self love, away from your Spirit.

Personal perception or imperfection perception personal beliefs about ourselves, others and the world that influences the way in which we interact in the world, how we play with others and what we think about ourselves. It directs our beliefs about our limitations, creates the life we have today, they are the glasses we wear to filter our life.

Spirit your true essence, the perfect self expression of you when connected to Source, God, Universe, the you born into this world.

Source, God, Universe, All that IS, Mother Earth are spiritual terms referring to a Source greater than ourselves. This is not a book on religion, but a spiritual book. You choose the term, word or phrase you feel most comfortable with that best describes a 'force' greater than yourself.

Our divine purpose is to live from a place of love in self love, to live our Spirit, share our gifts and talents with all of creation, to live our highest good, to live that which calls us, to love ourselves and each other unconditionally, to be happy!

An excellent way to begin connecting with your Spirit, to experience the joy and love of Divine Purpose, is to give back and share your gifts in some capacity that speaks to your Spirit. As you experience the joy of giving of your time and talents, you begin to open up, you begin to feel more love in the joy of giving and you receive even more love in return. As we give we feed our Spirit. As we give we feed the lives of those receiving. Those receiving return gratitude to us and they continue the flow of sharing, giving and receiving, as we are all connected. *'Giving is as important as receiving. Receiving is as important as giving; this is the energetic flow of abundance in action'.* We keep the flow moving to maintain a balanced life, living in this beautiful flow of connection, sharing, love, appreciation, gratitude and peace. It all begins with loving yourself, living in your heart from a place of love. Loving yourself opens you to loving others and receiving love back from others.

We have just discussed what self love is and demonstrated why it is fundamental to living a life of purpose. We have learned that the answers in the search for love come from within us; we create our own solid foundation for a fulfilling, happy life, from the inside out. Now let us move on to the 'wakeup call', the messages we receive when an area(s) of our life is no longer working for us.

Waking Up
In Your Head

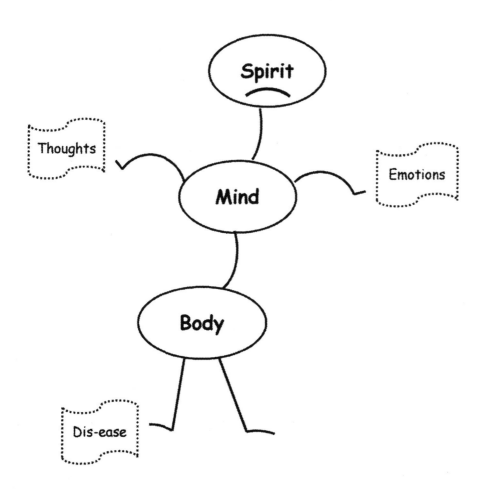

Chapter 2

The Wakeup Call

Whose life is this?

Why am I so Stressed?

Why am I so Unhappy?

Why do my relationships keep failing?

Why do I lose weight only to gain back even more?

Why is there never enough money?

If you find yourself asking these questions or making any of these statements it may be your wakeup call! These are messages, an alarm signal, from your Spirit that you are not living true to your Self, true to your Spirit. Take a moment to read through the following and feel if you can identify with any of these questions and statements:

"Is this all there is?" I have reached my perceived successes professionally, in my career, now what? I am turning a milestone age 30, 40, 50, 60 or 70, am I were I want to be? My family and spouse are content, but what about me? I have accomplished many goals and consider myself successful, but I still feel there

is something lacking or missing from my life, like there is more for me to do.

"Now what?" The kids are grown and have their own lives, I feel lost, I need to fill my days. My spouse pasted away, I need to create a new life, I need direction. I am divorced, I have my life back, no more compromise, but what do I want to do? I was laid off (or retired), my career gave me my identity, who am I now?

"What is my purpose?" No matter how much I achieve I still feel empty, unhappy, not fulfilled, like there should be more.

"What do I want to do with my life?" I know I can do anything I want, but what do I want? What do I like, How can I make money doing what I like?

"What do I want to be when I grow up?" (This was my personal mantra for about 40 years!) I have tried everything to find contentment and purpose, I am stuck. I have had an intellectual career, a creative career, no career, no money, I have had money, opportunity, possessions, but something is missing, I am bored, I do not feel happy.

This is the 'wakeup call' that you are living in your head.

You have disconnected from your heart, your Spirit.

You have disconnected from your feelings.

You are living not in your Heart from a place of Love, but

In your Head where fear, lack and ego live.

When you wake up one day and say *"I am not happy, or my life is not fun or fulfilling"* or worse you wake up one day feeling physically ill or are diagnosed with a life threatening illness, you are receiving messages from your Spirit to your mind and body. These messages are an alarm that you are out of Balance, the disconnection from your Spirit mind and body has become too great and it is time for a change. The messages if ignored will continue to grow louder threatening more serious consequences until you pay attention and the appropriate changes are made! When ignored the magnitude of the message will increase from being unhappy, into the loss of a job, or into loss of a relationship, a stomach ache, may turn into ulcers and the messages will continue until you pay attention and make a change.

The day we get that wakeup call is a joyful day because we are awakening, becoming conscious. The messages our Spirit is sending are being received and we can now spring into action, change what we want to change, change what no longer serves our highest and best self.

Our external circumstances are a reflection of our internal thoughts and beliefs. When we find ourselves living someone else's life, we need to examine our life, we will recognize the influences of our parents', teachers', society, cultures' and organized religions'. Recorded in our programming are their beliefs and perceptions about what we should be, how we should act, how we should think and feel, we have forgotten our connection, our spirit, our desires, we are not living our life but someone else's version of what they think our life should be. *We receive a wakeup call when we have drifted too far away from our Spirit, when the gap between the life we are living is* *no longer in harmony with the life we were meant to live.* Our Spirit sends the message to us that we are out of balance, by making our lives uncomfortable or even painful. The wakeup call can come in many forms, if you are fortunate to be more in tune with your feelings; you may just have the nagging feeling of emptiness or boredom even though your life is 'okay'. If you have ignored the more subtle messages, you may receive a life changing call such as the diagnosis of a life threatening illness, the loss of a job, or divorce.

We know when our life is not working, deep down inside we know. Ask yourself, "Are you happy?" Right now this minute are your completely fulfilled, joyous and pleased with yourself in all that you do, say and have?

Situations, relationships and questions arise in our lives that can cause major shifts in comfort levels for us personally; often these shifts affect those around us, signaling that change is coming. These situations or changes in comfort levels often manifest themselves as stress and anger. When we receive these signals of discontent, it is welcomed because that means we are waking up! Whatever we are currently doing no longer resonates with who we are now, it is time to re-examine our life. Are we feeding our Spirit in a way that fills us with joy and purpose?

The messages we receive from our spirit cause us to be uncomfortable if we are out of balance in Spirit mind and body. *The messages from our spirit are similar to an alarm; there is meaning in the discomfort, a signal trying to catch our attention.* This discomfort can take many forms, in many different situations but the underlying discomfort is the same. When we find ourselves stressed, ill, or unhappy experiencing uncomfortable emotions, unhappy feelings or destructive behavior, such as addictions, we are receiving messages from our Spirit, these are alarm signals. Our Spirit, our true essence, from our heart is communicating to us that we are out of balance and a change is necessary, the sooner the better! Our Spirit will signal us though our emotions when our current behavior does not resonate with our heart, our true spirit. When our actions and thoughts do not feel true to who we are now and no longer serves our higher good, our Spirit generates a negative emotional reaction inside of us. These messages deserve our full attention. If our Spirit is not taken seriously and ignored, our Spirit will send more serious messages that may result in health issues, loss of job, loss of income, loss of relationships. The ultimate function of our Spirit Mind Body is to protect us; keep us from fear and pain, guide us to love and happiness, these messages keep us in balance.

The messages from our Spirit take many forms. They are always well intentioned, always for our highest good, communicated to protect us. We appreciate the messages from our Spirit when we hold in mind that all our life experiences are to be perceived as positive lessons that support our growth, lifting us up to a higher level. *The messages we receive from our Spirit all have positive intentions and emotions are the vehicle in which these messages are sent.* For example when we experience a situation not in harmony with our current desires, a feeling of stress, anger or sadness is usually an emotional signal that something is not right, not 'resonating' with us in our current present day life. Something, a situation, a behavior, or a person may no longer serve or support us in attaining our higher good, so an emotion arises, anger, sadness, causing a feeling of stress.

One form of message from Spirit is when we find ourselves in situations in which we feel we cannot control the outcome, we feel fear. *Feeling that something is 'done to us', or that 'we are wronged', that we are a victim, are emotions generated out of fear from the head and ego.* We choose how we want to react in every situation. We may choose to play the victim role or we may choose to acknowledge that the other person has issues. We must accept that we only have control over our own feelings, actions and reactions; we cannot control another person's thoughts, feeling, actions, or reactions. The other person may see their behavior as justified unaware how it is affecting us. Because we each choose how we feel based on our past experiences, each of us is drawing from and acting on *our* personal past experience. Remember *'personal perception'* or *'personal imperfection'?* For example in a situation of an unsolicited favor, let us examine the perceptions involved: John decides to take an action in which he feels he is doing a favor for Mary, or doing what he thinks is a positive behavior that will benefit Mary, however Mary is angry because she did not ask for the favor, so John feels he is a victim, unappreciated, and Mary feels the emotion of fear, believing that she is seen as weak, not capable of doing for herself. As we know, each of us draw from our past experiences and perceptions which form our current behaviors and beliefs.

During our human experience *we must always believe that we always act to the best of our current ability based on our current knowledge.* We must believe we make the best possible choices with the current information and knowledge that is available to us. But we have to take responsibility for ourselves, our actions and our life. We are responsible for creating our own lives; we choose how we act and how we feel. When we feel that something is done to us and we play the victim, we are giving away our power to another. When we play the victim we are in fear giving away control of our situation. Playing the victim and feeling helpless creates a very dangerous level of fear, anger and stress, this combination is a recipe for a life threatening illness.

We create our own happiness; we choose how we want to feel about any given situation. It is our interpretation of an event, filtered in through our perceptions and personal lies, that results in a thought, the thought is given energy with our emotions, ultimately creating our behavior. We choose how we think, feel and act. Our present day experiences are being filtered through our perception in our subconscious mind. Our subconscious mind is matching our new experiences with our past experiences. The subconscious will interpret or perceive a current situation based on the past experiences. Past experiences have been recorded and programmed into our subconscious. If a program in our subconscious is no longer true for us, or we desire a new outcome, when a new desirable experience is processed, and rejected, an alarm signal creates dis-ease or we become un-balance. When our desires and limiting beliefs conflict, no longer resonate with us, our Spirit will generate a message that result in the form of an emotion, we feel unhappy, uncomfortable, and angry causing us stress.

Another situation that will cause us great stress is when we live in the past or future, Spirit will send a message that we are out of balance. *When we live in the past we live with regret, guilt, shame of what we should have done, when we live in the future we worry what might happen.* When we live in the past and future we miss the present moment. Living in the present moment, right now, we are present, we are aware in this moment, we do not regret the past, nor worry in the future. We just enjoy the *now*, experiencing the fullness of what we are currently doing or focusing on. Living in the now gives us peace of mind because there is no emotional baggage of the past and no anxiety for future events, just the peace of now, the rich full experience of the *now*.

Messages of illness or dis-ease are unexpressed emotions, energy trapped inside your body waiting to be released. Awareness of emotions is half the solution to decreasing stress. As you will read later, deeper awareness of your emotions will help you make sense of why you feel the way you do, raising your awareness allowing for the change of limiting beliefs. Connecting with your emotions and your feelings will reduce stress, supporting your body into better health.

These are just a few examples of how our Spirit communicates with our mind and body that it is necessary to make a change, a warning alarm before we are too far out of balance and serious damage occurs. Change requires the willingness to listen to your Spirit, begin by changing your thoughts and your actions will follow. To change how we 'feel' we must change our thoughts from negative to positive. We focus on the new positive thoughts and turn them into positive emotions; this creates new positive beliefs and behaviors.

Your interpretations of an event through your thoughts, or perception, in your mind create an emotional reaction in your body. Let us examine the components that keep us in balance, the connection between your Spirit Mind and Body.

The Spirit Mind Body Connection

What is Spirit?

Your Spirit is you, your true authentic self, your true essence. Your Spirit is the essence of who you really are. Your Spirit intuitively knows what you love to do, how you want to be in this world, what your divine purpose is. To live your Spirit you live from your heart, from a place of love, in the present moment. When you live your Spirit, you live from a place of self love, fulfilled and connected to your inner wisdom, connected to Source, God, All that Is.

What is Mind?

Your mind creates your thoughts. Your mind creates the emotions to add energy to those thoughts. Your mind controls your body; your body reacts to your thoughts and emotions, which ultimately create your reality. Your mind, generating your thoughts and emotions, is responsible for the current life you have, your reality, and your current health. Your thoughts are your perception of your reality in life. Your thoughts originate in your mind, left unguarded; your mind attaches emotions to your thoughts to give your thoughts even more power. You give your thoughts motion with emotion attracting more of what you think about, negative or positive. Your thoughts and emotions control your behavior, your decisions, your success, your happiness, your health, your life, your current reality. *Your mind manifests what you think about with no regard to 'Fact or Fiction'. Your mind complies with your wishes, what you dwell on is made true for you by your loyal, faithful, trusted well meaning companion, your mind.*

**Awareness of your thoughts allows
choice of actions and reactions.**

<u>Mind</u> = *Thoughts + Emotions*

What is Body?

Your body is a reflection of what you think and feel on the inside. Your body is a physical example of all your thoughts and emotions. The body is either in balance and harmony or is un-balanced in dis-ease. When our body is in a stress mode, it is out of balance with our Spirit our 'true' essence. When we are out of balance in stress mode, we are living and acting in ways that no longer serve our best self, no longer resonate with our Spirit. When our body is in healing, healthy relaxed mode, it is in balance, in harmony with our Spirit, our Mind, with our thoughts and emotions.

Out of Balance / Dis-ease = Body = In Balance / Health

Stress * Overload   Relax * Harmony

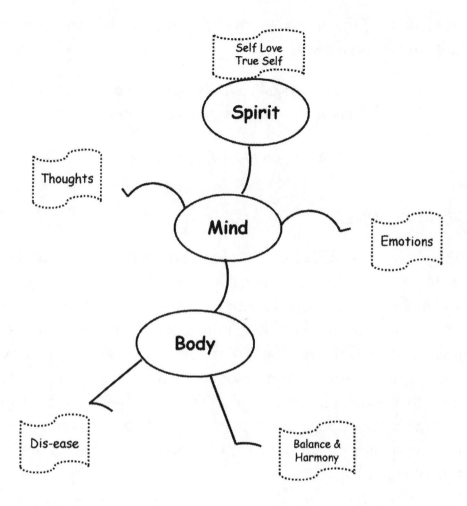

We are born connected, living from the heart, from our Spirit in pure love with a natural knowing of what is true for us. We receive a wakeup call, a message from our Spirit, when our current life is in danger of dragging us too far away from our true self, we are drifting too far out of balance away from who we truly are deep down inside. The message will cause discomfort, an alarm that an area(s) in our life is no longer in harmony with what is true for us. How did this disconnect happen? Did we just wake up one morning and find that we were living someone else's life? Have we been unconscious, sleep walking for the last 20 or 30 years?

Chapter 3

How did I get Disconnected?

How do we get disconnected from our source? When a baby is born it is innocent, connected to Spirit, Source, God, Universe. The baby knows no fear, the baby just 'is'. We start out as beautiful, creative, joyful, loving, spirits. As our disconnect from our Spirit, our Source, grows over the years we find ourselves feeling more alone, feeling unworthy, in fear, and unhappy.

We move from living from our hearts, from a place of love, to living in our heads from a place of fear and ego. The journey from our heart to our heads occurs as we travel along our life path and begin to experience the influences of outside sources. In the beginning, viewed through the eyes of children we accept authority figures and peers influences on our perceptions as our truth. The disconnect continues to grow as we alter our vision of ourselves as we mature from infants into children. We no longer see and feel that pure innocence of perfection, we willingly accept other people's ideas and opinions as our own, we decide to apply their personal perceptions to ourselves, making this our truth! To compound matters we decide that the emotions from our heart are not acceptable or safe to express. When we create a fear of our emotions, we commit to a life time of negative energy by holding back what we feel, stuffing down and burring our spirit, creating illness, dis-ease and overall unhappiness!

The disconnect from source continues gradually, day by day, as we turn from love to fear. The outside perceptions influencing the truth we decided about ourselves from the approximate young ages of two through seven. Some believe that we are subject to outside influences before we are even born. The belief is that an unborn child is affected by both negative and positive energy vibrations in the womb because we are all connected through energy vibration. The outside influences that mold our perception during ages two through seven are in the form of family, parents, teachers, religious figures, culture, peers, and society, all of those that as children we see as authority figures. These authority figures are the people we expect to love us, to appreciate us, to see the good in us. We decide and accept our truths, or personal lies, as a protection mechanism. In later years as an adolescents and adults if we experience a trauma or major drama we will program this into our subconscious too. The mission of the negative limiting belief's programming into our subconscious mind is to protect us from future pain and uncomfortable emotions. Our subconscious has only the best of intentions for us, to protect us from what we decided was too painful or too uncomfortable to experience again.

Our basic programming at that young age is written into our subconscious mind and we continue to use this same program to create our life into present day. These limiting beliefs, or personal lies, we decided about ourselves are written in our subconscious programming and will remain there until we reprogram them. Even though we may know intellectually, or feel differently now, our subconscious mind functions as if on auto pilot, filtering new ideas and situations through the original program. The subconscious mind accepting only what new ideas and situations match old programming, throwing current day into the results of past experiences, with no allowance for a different outcome, rejecting new ideas and experiences that do not fit into past programming.

For a visual of this process, imagine today at your current age, walking through life wearing a pair of glasses that only allow you to view current circumstances through the eyes of a two to seven year old. Please take a moment if you will and image being about five years old. Now as a five year old imagine a recent conversation, or disagreement, you were involved in, perhaps this was with a boss, a co-worker or spouse, that did not turn out as well as you had planned. The wisdom and emotional maturity of a two to seven year old is actually creating and making decisions in your life today, creating your reality. Is it surprising that you may find yourself unhappy and puzzled by your current life, the life you created through the 'imperfection perception' of a child?

Our disconnect from our Spirit, Source, God creates lack of self love, we forget we were born perfect, the essence of pure love. This disconnect manifests problems and struggles in all areas of our life, in our relationships, in our career, and in our health. Disconnected, lacking in self love results in the feeling of being alone, unworthy and unhappy. As we discussed earlier, the lack of self love finds us looking outside of ourselves for love, looking to others to make us happy or for approval. We know the opposite of Love is Fear. When we are disconnected, we live from a place of fear in our head; our ego generates thoughts to protect us. Thoughts of judgment and resentment begin to take hold. We play the role of victim in our life, we feel everything happens *to* us, we feel we have no control, we blame others, we feel our problems in life are not our fault. As a victim, not taking responsibility for our lives, we create an unsatisfying life. As a victim we create health issues through the stress of feeling that we have no control, the anger of resenting others, feeling we are never good enough, or judging others so we feel superior. The victim role is a low energy vibration so we attract more of exactly what we do not want, more negative results and more negative situations!

The Ego is part of us, and we need to acknowledge it, be aware of it and put the ego in the proper role. *The ego mind creates all of our stress and unhappiness*, the ego uses fear to fuel our emotions. *Fear is no more than our perception of a situation.* The ego is the negative part of us that has to make others wrong so we are right, so that we feel good about ourselves, until we feel bad about our actions and then beat ourselves up about it and then our ego beats us up about beating ourselves up! *Round and round the ego goes, it will never stop. Know that the ego is never satisfied, it never stops.* Fear and ego are the voice in your head that is always negative, living in the past 'should have's', and living in the future 'what if's'. The ego never lives in the present moment. So, if you want to live in peace and contentment, just live in the now, more on that later!

There is a story about a group of children about the ages of seven gathered on a grammar school playground. This story represents an example of coming from a place of fear and ego, making others wrong or made to feel inferior, in order to feel better about themselves, and personal lies we decide about ourselves. The cast includes a bully and several unconscious supports, a girl who decided to accept society's opinions of unacceptable weight and height, and a girl who acted out in anger. There was a lead bully shouting cruel, unkind remarks on the playground, to whoever would listen, while laughing with several other boys about the physical height and weight of a girl who stood alone on a crowded playground. The bully was enjoying his moments of attention, making himself feel good, feeling superior, and enjoying the pain he was causing this young girl. Another young girl appeared, approaching the bully in anger, demanding that he stop his cruel words and actions immediately; she was about the same height and weight as the girl who stood alone, crying. Apparently ready to show him the error of his misguided ways, armed with a folded umbrella, this angry girl seemed to be a pretty good match for the bully as she began chasing him. The running continued for some minutes as she chased the bully around the playground waving the folded umbrella in the air in a passionate fit of anger, attempting to catch him, possibly inflicted some pain and embarrassment upon him. Before any physical confrontation resulted recess was called to an end.

Let us take a moment here to imagine the possibilities of the programming that may have occurred in the subconscious mind of each of the cast members of this event. This story is an example of both subconscious programming and the philosophy that *the characters in this scene were each doing the best they could with the information they had at the time.* The Bully, perhaps he was emotionally teased by his father or older brothers. To the bully teasing or to 'pick on' someone, was a sign of attention, a sign of love, after all his family members loved him and would never harm him or cause him pain, right? Or perhaps the Bully did feel pain and wanted to lash out at another so he would not feel alone in his pain, wanted others to join him in his pain. Perhaps he would feel connected or loved? The girl who was being verbally abused may have decided that the bully was correct; she was ugly, not worthy of love, but someone to be made fun of, someone who is not good enough. Or was it a sign of affection, of love, if you are noticed, singled out with attention, any kind of attention, negative or positive is love right? For the girl with the umbrella, perhaps she felt the needed to lash out in anger because she too decided that she was unworthy because of her size. Or did she feel the need to rescue the underdog, a need to lend assistance even though not solicited, to make her feel worthy, of value, to be needed is to be loved, to help is to be appreciated, is to be loved true?

Perception for Protection

We decide what is true for us,
it becomes our limiting belief

Remember each child in the story was creating their own 'perception for protection', the perception we decide upon is what is true for us, these become our limiting beliefs. Our subconscious mind protects us from hurt and pain by generating thoughts filtered though our perception at the time of the event. Thoughts create emotions. The combination of thoughts and strong emotions create a 'Belief' that we decide is true for us, this goes into our program to be used as a filter for future situations. The ego steps in to create 'stories' to make us feel better. Our personal stories, what we decided about ourselves at young ages, become are the personal 'lies'. We carry our personal lies all thorough our lives until, if ever, we decide to change them.

We all carry these stories with us from childhood into maturity. We make our decisions in present day based on what we decided is true for us when we were children. Today we may or may not even be aware that we are carrying around a false belief that limits us from achieve our full potential. Many of us walk around unconscious; unaware of why we do things that sabotage our success. We rarely ask ourselves questions about our beliefs, "Is this true? Why do I believe that? Where did that opinion come from? Who do I sound like when I say that?"

We are the result of the programming in our subconscious mind. We develop ideas, behavior and beliefs about ourselves that cause us pain, limit our success, and no longer serve our needs. Why is it that no matter how much willpower we use, no matter how intelligent we are, we are usually unsuccessful at changing negative, limiting or self destructive behaviors, thoughts or beliefs? For programming or reprogramming to take place in the subconscious mind several factors must be present. An event takes place with high emotion attached to it, right then we decide something, this creates a belief. The belief then drives a behavior which creates results into our life.

Event + Emotion = Belief = Behavior = Results

An Event happens, for example a reprimanded by an authority figure in front of peers at school or an event is repeated many times, for example physical abuse at the hand of a parent. High emotion is added to the event; especially high emotion allows programming or reprogramming of the subconscious mind to take place. Then a belief is decided. Our conscious mind receives input from this event, the input passes through our filter into the subconscious mind. The subconscious mind decides what to believe based on previous experiences; it accepts this new input and checks it with existing beliefs. The subconscious mind will say 'yes this is true' if the belief is already in our program or the subconscious rejects the input because there is not a matching belief in the existing program. What we are today, how we behave, what we think and feel, and what we have created into our lives, is a result of this programming process. This program process creates our personal truth, this is the program that runs how we act and interact, what we think about ourselves and others, how we go through this life experience. The lack of self love is the cause of all emotional pain and most likely the catalyst of all physical pain and illness.

Our mind runs our everyday routine, like computer software, on auto pilot, accepting, rejecting filtering and comparing previous experiences. Our conscious mind is responsible for choice, logic, will and our five senses. What comes in as a belief that is either true or not true for us is filtered by a part of the conscious mind. Our subconscious mind stores these beliefs. We access the subconscious mind to reprogram our outdated beliefs and perceptions that no longer serve our higher purpose. The subconscious mind, also referred to as the unconscious mind, has a big job. The subconscious mind controls our Autonomic Nervous System which is responsible for generating our fight or flight response. The subconscious mind controls our emotion, imagination, belief and memory storage. **The subconscious mind does not discern fact from fiction.**

> ## _Thoughts + Emotions = Behavior_
>
> ### _MIND creates thoughts BODY creates reaction_
>
> ### _Sympathetic = Stress_   _Parasympathetic = Relax_

The autonomic nervous system has two responses, '_Sympathetic_' and '_Parasympathetic_'. The sympathetic, or Stress Response, is also known as the fight or flight response. Our body is in protect mode when responding to stress. There are two types of stress, acute stress, the sudden or occasional surge of stress, and chronic stress, a continued stress response in the body. _Chronic stress is the unnecessary danger to our health which we create._ Chronic stress causes many serious health issues, such as heart disease and high blood pressure to name a few. Chronic stress suppresses the immune system, making it difficult for our body to protect itself from illness.

The second response of the autonomic nervous system is the parasympathetic response. This is the body's safety response or health mode. In this state the body is relaxed, maintains 'homeostasis', a balanced state. When the body is relaxed, healing with more rapid results is possible, the immune system has time to restore and heal were healing is necessary. Calm supports the body in healing, unlike the protecting mode which is triggered by stress. The ingredients of stress, are negativity, fear and worry, the ingredients of health are positive thoughts, love and calm.

With the power of our mind we create thoughts; thoughts combined with emotions generate energy attracting more of whatever we think about or focus on. Our reality is a direct creation originated in our thoughts. What we decided to be true about us and our perceptions of the world create our relationships, careers, income and our health. Lack of self love is at the core of all painful living, emotional and physical.

To reconnect back to self love we need to clear the clutter in our subconscious mind. To reconnect we first change the false beliefs we decided about ourselves as we tried to protect ourselves from pain as children. We begin to let go of the negative defensive ego, let go of the lies of being unlovable, unworthy, not good enough, let go of the fear.

We are a balanced unit, consisting of three components, our Spirit, our Mind and our Body all three aspects of our being, energetically connected, balanced and functioning as one harmonious unit. Energetically we are connected to our source and other energies such as the animals and the people around us. The connection with our spirit is pure love. When in balance we live from a place of love, we live from our hearts; we are connected to our Spirit, God, Source, all creation and people. We are born with a knowing, without limitation in our imagination and spiritual energy, with unlimited anticipation and expectation of all things possible.

The beauty of our Spirit is that our connection is always within us, it never goes away, we just need to remember and re-connect with it! Instinctually as infants and young children we desire to be loved. As young children we have vivid imaginations, pretending that we are super heroes, doctors, nurses, teachers, firemen.

Our imagination is still available to us, we are the creators of our own lives, we create our reality, we decide, we choose what type of life we desire, either consciously or unconsciously. The great news is that you can change your life at anytime by changing your thoughts. By creating a new reality, replacing negative thoughts with positive ones, you will immediately begin to attract more good into your life. So you decide, you get to choose how you want your life to be. *Congratulations!* Now that you are awake, you can choose to change your life! You can create a new reality by changing your thoughts and powering them with emotion.

Chapter 4

My Reality, My Responsibility

> **You create your reality!**
>
> **What your life is today is a creation of**
>
> **Your Thoughts and Your Actions**
>
> **Thoughts = Reality**

How do you change your reality? We start by taking responsibility for our life, only then can we begin to create the life we desire. Create a new reality. Why do we stay disconnected, stuck for so long, when changing our life is as easy as changing our thoughts? Fear! *Fear of the unknown is more painful than the unhappy life we are currently living.* Being unhappy, staying stuck is easier because it is safe, we know this life, and in a backward way, the pain is more comfortable than the fear of reaching for happiness and failing, or worse yet, succeeding! What would we do if we actually achieved and received all we desired? Could we handle it? From a place of Love yes, from a place of Fear no.

For positive change the first step is to accept responsibility for your life, responsibility for your choices and responsibility for the current life you have created. Accept the responsibility that you decide, you choose; you create your own reality. Accept that you no longer play the role of a victim in your own life.

When you accept responsibility for your life you take back your power. When you take responsibility for your current life you can begin to change your reality, by changing your perceptions, changing your self talk from negative to positive, replace limiting beliefs with positive energy thoughts, your actions become higher energy, you begin to attract more good into your life, you begin to create the life you desire, a new reality.

We must make the commitment to ourselves to take responsibility for our thoughts; we must be willing and want change for affirmations, prayer, meditation, and self hypnosis to be effective in supporting positive change. Positive affirmations must be believable or positive change will not occur. To pray without faith or sincerity, or to meditate and only think about a grocery list will not produce effective results. The same is true for hypnosis, if you are not willing, self hypnosis will not be effective.

Your mind is a wonderful tool for creating emotional and physical healing and health. When you change negative beliefs into positive beliefs, you begin to change your thoughts. By changing your thoughts you change your emotions. When your emotions are calm and positive they support health. Calm healthy emotions change the reactions in your body; the result is improved health, complete Spirit, Mind, Body balance and harmony.

To change your reality, you must feel a strong emotional desire and believe change is possible.

- ✓ Think the New Positive Thought
- ✓ Feel and Desire the New Positive Outcome
- ✓ Believe the New Positive Outcome is your New Reality
- ✓ Expect and Anticipate Your New Reality

Once we have accepted responsibility for our thoughts, we are ready to move on to the practice of creating and maintaining positive thoughts and actions. We adopt the attitude that we are open and receptive to all good things coming our way. We raise our thoughts to expect good things to happen to us, we begin to expect only the best for our lives. We create a belief of anticipation for the arrival of our best and highest good, what we desire. *Expectation and anticipation are like magnets attracting whatever we think about into our lives.* Expectation and anticipation attract more of whatever we focus on. We attract more good, or more bad, into our life in direct relationship to our thoughts.

Our thoughts are so powerful that when left uncontrolled, or *while being unaware of our thoughts, we continue to have the ability to bring more of what we did not consciously ask for into our life!* As your awareness of your thoughts grows the minute you have a negative thought you almost panic, not wanting to manifest any negative into your life. A fun technique to use when you think a negative thought is to immediately say to yourself, or out loud, "cancel, cancel" or 'out of here'. When we become conscious of our thoughts, taking responsibility for them, we truly begin to appreciate their power, knowing that if you image and believe a thought, you can manifest almost anything into your life.

A wonderful example to demonstrate the power of our thoughts is to call on our imagination and think of a fresh lemon, in your mind smell the skin, feel the texture with your fingers, using your imagination, take a sharp knife and cut into the lemon, see the juice on the cutting board, smell the citrus aroma. Take a section of the lemon in your hand the juice running down your fingers onto your hand, bite into the lemon wedge. Can you feel the tingle of your salivary glands? Are you experiencing more saliva in your mouth? Just from your thoughts you have created a response in your body! This is without any physical action, your thoughts created a reaction in your body. *Imagine what you would be able to accomplish if you consciously, intentionally, created your thoughts?* Talk about all things possible, unlimited possibilities, the sky is the limit!!

Reprogramming takes place in your subconscious mind, this is where and when positive changes take place! Our mind reacts to images and suggestions, we do not actually have to physically do the motion, just thinking about an image or suggestion, our subconscious will react. Our subconscious does not distinguish fact from fiction.

> **The subconscious mind does not distinguish between fact and fiction**
>
> **Create your thoughts = Create your reality = Create your health**

Accepting responsibility for our thoughts begins to raise our awareness of the type of thoughts we are having. *If you can think it you can achieve it!* A life of happiness, bliss, joy, peace, contentment, fulfillment, purpose, loving relationships, and abundance begins with changing your thoughts. Awareness of our thoughts is the foundation to creating positive change. Awareness of thoughts is conscious living, living in the now, allowing you to create the life you desire.

Chapter 5

Awareness of Spirit Mind Body

Living in awareness, or conscious living, is being present in your life while you are living it. *Awareness is being awake, living in the moment, participating in your life while your life is happening. You make your life happen, it is not happening to you.* Awareness is also self awareness, tuning into every thought, feeling, and action in the now, in the moment you are living it. Awareness is conscious living making conscious choices of your every thought, feeling and action. Awareness of Spirit, Mind and Body brings perfect balance and harmony to your life.

Awareness is similar to a concentrated focus on the task at hand or the action you are performing right now, this minute. For example awareness in washing the dishes would be to feel the temperature of the water, feel the soap as slippery and see the sudsy bubbles, see the glass grow shinier as you wipe it with the dish cloth, feel the weight of the glass in your hand, as you rinse the glass watch the soapy water runoff, you get the idea. *One of the most amazing benefits of conscious awareness, focusing on the task at hand, is that time is stretched.* I find that when I need to make more time I just focus my awareness on the task at hand and I have plenty of time to accomplish what I need to accomplish.

Awareness of Spirit

Does this feel true?

In the moment awareness, of what is 'true' for you, is the practice of checking in with yourself. Living your Spirit, living from a place of love can also be described as *Living Your True Self, Living your Authentic Self, Living in Awareness* or *Conscious Living, Living an Enlightened Life.* Awareness is tuning into your spirit, your inner voice, your higher self, your intuition. The more you practice awareness and conscious living the more you will hear and learn to act on your intuition or inner voice. Your inner voice is your true self, your spirit, communicating with you. Your inner voice speaks your higher wisdom. Your higher wisdom speaks the answers that are true for you, the answers found deep inside of you, the inner knowing deep in your heart, in your spirit. Your inner voice is always available to you, always available to guide you in the right direction whenever you choose to be aware and listen. The practice of hearing your inner voice, then acting on what your inner voice is guiding you to do, is the process of reconnecting with your true self, the process of awakening your spirit. Waking up, living in the awareness of what is true for you, feeling your feelings and choosing to act on these feelings, is what reconnects you to your Spirit.

As we develop greater awareness we continue the journey from our head back to our heart. We develop conscious living by tuning into how we feel, what feels true for us. Our truth feels comfortable; our truth feels calm and natural, flowing. Un-truth, or not living our Spirit, feels forced, we feel anxious, we feel a little concern, we feel fear. The opposite of Love is Fear. Both love and fear are perceptions; we have the choice to choose a thought fueled with either corresponding emotion fear or love. When you live your Spirit, you live in the flow of life, you feel calm and relaxed. Fear is fueled by the ego which lives in your head.

Living in Awareness leads to living our truth, living our Spirit or true self, living from a place of love, living in self love. Self love is loving and accepting you as you are, a perfect expression of you, accepting that you are a divine creation, a spirit of light and energy that is beautiful and perfect in every way.

As we raise our awareness we begin to love and appreciate ourselves and others more. We appreciate our many talents, becoming more aware of all that we have accomplished and all that we are capable of contributing into the world in which we live. We begin to appreciate the many gifts we have available to us and our desire to share these gifts with others increases. We become more grateful for all that we have. To love and accept ourselves without judgment and fear allows our Spirit to be open to truly love and accept others without judgment and fear.

Living your Spirit in awareness connects you with your passion. Living your Spirit you will re-discover your divine purpose, living a happy, peaceful, joyful, blissful, abundant, and prosperous life. Does this sound like something you are interested in creating in your life? Are you ready to create the life you desire?

Claim your highest good, claim your passion, your perfect self expression. Spirit, God, Source, Universe are waiting to deliver your gifts to you, right now!! Yours for the asking. But, you have to ask. You have to claim your good by attracting your good to you! The upside is that to have all you desire, to have purpose, abundance, fulfillment, is a simple process! The challenge is that it takes your sincere desire and willingness to participate in, and commit to, the daily practices' that will help and guide you toward greater self love and living your Spirit.

Fear + Logic + Ego = Ego Based Guidance

Love + Feels Right = Spirit Based Guidance

Awareness of Mind

Is this true for me?

Awareness, conscious living, or Living in the Moment allows you to be aware of each negative and positive thought as you are experiencing them. Awareness in the moment allows you to catch the thought in that moment and ask yourself any or all of the following questions:

- ✓ Is this thought true for me now?
- ✓ Does this thought support me in my new desires?
- ✓ Does this thought feed my Spirit as a positive, uplifting message or is it a negative, personal lie?
- ✓ Is this thought loving and supportive of me?
- ✓ Does this thought support what I want to attract more of into my life?

Awareness also applies to emotions which we will examine further in the next chapter. As we discussed earlier emotions, give energy to our thoughts. *If we miss the negative thought, did not catch it in the moment it occurred, we can catch the emotion in awareness before it generates negative energy.*

When we consciously call on our mind to imagine, visualize and manifest all we desire for our highest good we are in a state of love, self love, happiness, joy and peace. Living from our Spirit connects us to our mind through the perception of love. When I think of viewing reality from the perception of love, the visual of rose colored glasses comes to mind. *Can you imagine experiencing all that we see, all that we feel and all that we do from a place of love, with the expectation of all positive results?* From a place of love anticipating all positive outcomes, all interactions with others are seen and felt as if others have our best interests at heart. The power of expectation and the power of anticipation are magnets that bring more good into our life.

Our mind is a wonderful, powerful, part of us that is available to us whenever we choose to utilize it. The full potential of the mind has not yet been realized. We possess many talents hidden away in our mind that we may not yet be aware of, skills that we posses but have forgotten how to use.

Our inner voice, higher wisdom, our intuition, is part of our internal guidance system that connects our Spirit, Mind and Body. When we live in awareness we begin to tune into our inner voice, our intuition. Gradually as we pay attention, we begin to listen more to our intuition. We begin to act on our inner voice, testing in a safe way with small steps. The more comfortable we are in listening to our higher wisdom, the more alive our Spirit becomes. Through awareness the communication grows between our Spirit, Mind, and Body creating a flow of calm and peace. Living from your Spirit, fear dissolves and the ego relaxes.

Awareness of Body

Where do I feel it?

With greater awareness we move from our heart into our body. When you are aware, in conscious living, your body responds immediately to your inner voice. In awareness we learn to tune in to our body and feel our body's reaction to our inner voice.

We feel from our heart and we feel from our body. The reaction to a thought or situation is often felt in the stomach area, or gut. Perhaps you have experienced 'butterflies in the stomach' at a time when you were nervous about a presentation or an ache in the stomach when facing an unpleasant situation. Feelings are part of your internal guidance system, feelings carry a message. Your intuition, or higher wisdom, is tuned into this guidance system. The more you are able to check in, or tune in, with your body through awareness, the more comfortable you will be relying on your inner voice, trusting your intuition, instead of staying in your head and listening to your ego.

Awareness allows you to 'tune in' and 'check in'. Tune in to your environment, what is going on around you, what is your reaction to others, what is your reaction to all that is happening outside of you. Tune in to others, how are others reacting to you, are you sending out positive energy? Awareness on the inside, check into what you are feeling, what words you are saying, what are your thoughts, what emotions are being generated. Tune in to how everything affects your body, ultimately your health, are you in dis–ease or harmony & balance?

The purpose of these questions is to bring the 'feeling' forward into your awareness. Once you are aware of the feeling, you are then able to acknowledge it and change your thoughts if you choose to do so.

Awareness—Consciously Create Your Reality

- ✓ Awareness of thoughts, self talk negative or positive
- ✓ Awareness of emotions what causes or triggers them
- ✓ Awareness of our words, support or tear down
- ✓ Awareness of our actions, behavior supportive or destructive
- ✓ Awareness of our environment, uncomfortable or comfortable
- ✓ Awareness of Others, family, associates, friends

In the journey toward self love, awareness begins to feel more comfortable and peaceful; you begin to know you are on the right path as life becomes less of a struggle, more in the flow. Living in awareness, catching a negative reaction or spoken untruth, helps to change the negative behavior. Living in awareness you choose exactly what you want to think and feel, creating the results you desire into your life. Awareness, living from the heart where our Spirit lives, living in self love, connects us to our mind where we create our thoughts, and connects our body where we create health. Awareness allows positive choices in thoughts and actions creating balance and harmony in Spirit, Mind Body, supporting self love and optimal health. Awareness opens the door for us to begin to acknowledge our emotions. Through awareness we begin to remove our fear and tune into our emotions and the feelings we generate.

Chapter 6

Emotions as Unexpressed Energy

Feelings are the Human Part of Us.

Feelings are the Intangible that makes our Life Tangible.

Feelings are Internal Energy that Connect Us to Our Physical World.

Our Six Senses Conduct and Transmit Feelings.

Emotions are the Energy of Feelings.

The Energy of our Emotions Flow Inside our Body.

Thought + Emotion = Behavior

We discussed earlier the concept of negative and positive thoughts, when powered by emotions, increase our ability to manifest our desires. Emotions are energy. The energy of emotions are felt all through our body. Our five senses, Hearing, Smell, Sight, Taste, and Touch, are the conduit from the outside to the inside of our body. Our sixth sense, call it intuition or energy awareness, is both an internal and external form of guidance transmitter. Our senses become aware and transmit signals of information. Our senses trigger a thought and a feeling response in the mind, a thought, perception, or memory causes the emotional energy reaction in the body. The following are examples of our six senses in action.

Hearing—we hear an argument, triggering a thought and feeling, we then become angry or remain calm. Hearing the laugh of a child brings a smile to our face, the feeling of happiness travels through our body.

Intuition or energy awareness—we sense energy vibrations and become alert to danger or remain at peace. With guidance from our Intuition we feel the calm knowing of a perfect decision made.

Sight—we see a situation that triggers a perception may make us anxious or remain confident. The sight of the sun sparkling on a crystal clear lake brings the feeling of appreciation of nature.

Smell—we may breathe in a scent that triggers a memory and become sad or remain happy. The smell of freshly cut lawn reminds us of a summer day as a child and the anticipation of adventure.

Taste—we trigger a perception as we decide either bitter or sweet. The taste of warm chocolate chip cookies bring comfort as the chocolate melts in your mouth.

Touch—we trigger a memory as we distinguish rough from smooth. The touch of silky puppy fur soft against your skin delivers contentment and relaxation.

Emotions are the sparks that make life tangible! *Emotions are the energy behind feelings.* Our thoughts generate feelings, feelings gain energy becoming emotions, and emotional energy circulates through our body until it is released. The ideal way to process an emotion is to feel it, acknowledge it, express it, and then the energy of the emotion passes through the body and is gone. When we have emotions that remain un-acknowledged and un-expressed, the emotions stay trapped in our body until we do express them. Un-acknowledged and un-expressed emotions directly affect our health both mentally and physically.

Not Allowing Emotions to be felt is like playing roulette with your health. Emotions are energy; this energy must be felt and expressed for a healthy balance of Spirit Mind Body. Emotions are signals from your Spirit Mind Body that you are out of balance in an area, or areas, of your life. Emotions are messages when ignored will persist; emotions will gain in strength each time they are sent until they are expressed. Imagine emotions as waves of energy moving through your body, carrying a message that must be heard. Your Spirit mind and body work together for you in harmony to protect you, your well being is the only objective, the mission is always to support your best interest, the natural process is to allow the energy of emotions to pass through your body. The message is sent, the emotion is felt, the message was received, and the job is done. Hopefully the message was received in awareness and received the attention it was requesting, making the appropriate changes to bring your life back into balance. Un-expressed emotions are unexpressed energy trapped in your body. Energy trapped in your body is a serious health risk. Energy blocks will manifest into serious health issues such as, cancer, heart disease, high blood pressure, migraine headaches, back pain, chronic pain, and the list continues.

The energy blocks of unexpressed emotions affect all aspects of your life, your relationships, your career and your finances. Blocked emotions, cause us to be out of balance. When we are out of balance our internal guidance is 'off'. When we are out of balance unhealthy choices may be made that cause additional stress or dis-ease, for example, in a relationship we may choose an unsuitable partner, in our workplace we may feel unappreciated, and in our finances we may make a rash decision. Emotions have to be released eventually, choosing the time and place to release this energy, in a way that would be most beneficial to you is a wise consideration.

Many of us are afraid of our emotions, so we choose not to express them. *The fact is the real fear of emotions is not having them; it is having them and not releasing them, or acknowledge them.* As we stated earlier emotions are like waves on the ocean, they come and go, and emotions are a natural part of the human experience. *Acknowledge what you are feeling, let it go and move on.*

Why are we afraid of our emotions? Are we afraid that once we feel and acknowledge an emotion we will not be able to control the feeling, control ourselves, as if we let a Genie out of a bottle? Are we afraid that we will like ourselves even less? Are we afraid that others will not like us when they see who we really are? *What Masks do you were?* What aspect of your personality or thoughts are you hiding deep inside you? What part of you are you afraid to acknowledge, or have others see, or know about? Is there a part of you inside that you are embarrassed of, or ashamed of? *The Shadow part of us is the part of us that we do not love, we hide it in fear, not wanting anyone to see or know about this part of us.*

What we do not like in others is usually a reflection of what we do not like in ourselves. Carl Jung referred to the unconscious mind as '*the shadow, its relentless efforts to discharge its contents as shadow projection* '. Our shadow self is usually the 'part(s)' of us we determine as undesirable or embarrassing, not necessarily what society says is 'wrong' or 'unacceptable', but what we deem unacceptable, our personal lies or untruths that we programmed into our subconscious mind as we discussed earlier. Our shadow parts are recorded in the program we run in our subconscious mind. As we know the subconscious mind runs our behaviors, thoughts, feelings, and emotions based on what we experienced and decided upon during the imprinting years of ages two through seven, or at later ages if there was a traumatic event.

These shadow emotions, thoughts and behaviors are what *we decided is wrong with us*, we decided we were unlovable or un-worthy, abandoned, ugly, stupid, so we work very hard to mask these emotions, to hide them, pretend they do not exist, we consider this our dark side. Shadow emotions live in a place of fear, not love.

This pretending or hiding of our emotions, thoughts and feelings, cause tremendous stress in our bodies, it takes a lot of energy to hold down the accumulated negative feelings of a lifetime. Imagine all of the stress energy we generate by stuffing down all the different aspects of our true Spirit, our true personalities, parts we do not want anyone to see, parts we are afraid of.

Our mind and body, performing their main objective to always support and protect us, will continue to generate all the energy necessary to help us keep pretending we are the personality we feel we need to be in various situations throughout the day. I think of the wizard behind the curtain in Oz with exaggerated motions and great fanfare generating the power necessary for our masks to function smoothly. Our mind and body are there to work for us, to keep our masks lit, to keep the engine of each personality running smoothly. Please take a moment to reflect, "How many masks do you wear in a day?" We have masks we wear for work, masks we put on for our family, and the masks we wear in social gatherings.

Mask, hats, or personalities, we are beautiful, perfect spirits in complex human minds and bodies experiencing emotions, utilizing our many gifts and methods of protection, we create multiple identities to successfully accomplish the task at hand, *we can be who we need to be when we need to be it!* Unfortunately the long term affects of wearing these masks is harmful to both our physical and mental health. It is like the cloaking device on a spaceship; it is effective but can drain the engines when used for a prolonged period of time! When we wear masks, or different personalities, hiding in fear because we do not love and appreciate this part of us, the energy generated is negative energy, which then becomes a part of our cells, literally part of our being. The stress of hiding this negative energy and fear manifests in our bodies as dis-ease, as mentioned earlier, high blood pressure, diabetes, cancer, migraines and chronic pain as just a few examples.

The process of changing these negative beliefs and thoughts begins with first recognizing and admitting what behaviors, feelings, and thoughts no longer resonate with us, no longer serve our highest good, that cause us pain, or sabotage our success. The second step is to acknowledge the value or lesson in the action and accept it. To accept a current belief, or situation, does not mean we agree with it, but it is necessary to acknowledge that it exists. *What we resist accepting, will continue to be present in our life until we accept it.* Resisting creates energy because emotion is involved in the resistance, therefore the energy is trapped in the body and will not go away until we accept and move on. We accept the situation and ask "What can I learn from this in creating my new desires, in achieving my higher good?" Third, we forgive ourselves and move on. Forgiving ourselves is important; we learn from the experience, it is in the past, we move in to the present. In the present moment there exists all new opportunity to attract what you desire for your new reality. Remember, we attract more of what we focus on. To move on we must decide to change and have the desire to change. We change by reaching our subconscious mind to reprogram our perceptions and beliefs that have been holding us back from our success, or good health, we replace the negative with positive thoughts changing our perception.

Example of recognizing, accepting, learning from, and changing a behavior that you now feel is limiting you from achieving your desired success:

You recognize and admit that your current behavior of being too agreeable, not voicing your true feelings, is a negative behavior. You accept that you do not know how to set limits, or say no, you are always doing for others, leaving no time for your own success or self care. You then forgive and appreciate yourself, learning the positive from this behavior, that you are very kind, caring and supportive of others. You move on by creating a positive change, setting healthy limits, saying no when necessary, allowing for your needs and your self care. Becoming aware of the limiting behavior of being 'too agreeable', accepting the lessons of setting limits and appreciating yourself as being kind, is the positive *change in your perception, allowing for greater self love*, eliminating the stress of not loving yourself and negative self talk.

The more aware we are of our feelings,

The more we love and appreciate ourselves.

When we love ourselves,

We are more open to love others;

We are more open to receive love from others.

Why is it so difficult to express emotions freely? The primary function of our emotions are to protect us, they are an internal guidance system and an alarm system. We must learn how to connect with and interpret our emotions. At a young age we decided it was inappropriate, or not safe, to express our emotions because we perceived that something undesirable, or bad, or painful, would happen. Today our life is still filtered through this original personal perception programming. We continue to filter our emotions through the program we created in our subconscious applying the wisdom and emotional maturity of a two to seven year old to present day decisions of what emotions must be held down and left unexpressed.

In the journey from our head back to our hearts as we develop a greater self love, we become more aware that *our emotions, as messages from our Spirit, are the ideal guidance system, for our emotions are spoken from the heart.* A loving message from our Spirit when received in awareness, felt and acknowledged is the connection to what we truly feel about an action, behavior, situation, thought or decision. When we tune into what is true for us, we feel calm, at peace with our actions and interactions, we flow through life, Spirit, mind, body in harmony and balance.

Tuning into our emotions is similar to an internal scan of our body. The moment you feel an emotion, stop, notice how you feel in your body, were you feel the emotion in your body, observe your energy level, and your internal vibration.

Your body responds immediately to an emotion. Emotions felt and acknowledged in self love, are positive high energy vibrations. Emotions from a place of love lead us to be aware and ask questions of our Spirit in calm, wondering manner, "Why do I feel sad hearing this? Why does this conversation make me uncomfortable?" Emotions felt in fear are negative, low in vibration. When the ego in our mind is at play, we are not in awareness. When we listen to our Spirit to guide us, we are listening to our inner voice, our intuition. *The answers are inside of us, all that we seek is inside of us. Who knows us better than our Spirit?*

As we tune in to our Spirit more and begin to trust our inner guidance we will gradually be able to let go of the negative voice in our head, our mind and ego speaking from fear. Greater awareness of our thoughts and emotions will lead us more and more to replacing negative with positives, creating our new positive personal perceptions and new positive behaviors to accomplish our new desires and goals.

Remember, we do not have to figure out exactly how to achieve what we desire, just know that you can achieve this or greater and believe your intentions with the highest emotion possible. Emotion is the fuel for successful manifesting. The only qualifier here is that *manifesting is always for the higher good of yourself and others.*

As we rediscover our connection to our Spirit, we become more comfortable with our emotions, accepting our emotions as they were intended, loving guidance from our Spirit, guidance that will support us in achieving happiness, joy, peace and abundance. We listen with gratitude to our heart as it speaks from a place of love. As we develop a greater self love, our Spirit mind and body come into harmony and balance.

From a Place of Love

As we know living from the heart is living from a place of love, appreciation and gratitude, the opposite being living in our head in fear and ego. When we love ourselves we come from a place of love, we are happy, we think positive thoughts; interact with others in a positive way for the best outcome, sending out higher energy attracting more of what we desire into our lives.

We contribute our gifts and talents, and in turn we are fulfilled living a life of purpose.

As we discussed earlier, true happiness comes from inside of us. External factors, possessions or persons cannot provide lasting happiness or make us truly happy. External influences can enhance our experiences and enrich our lives. Giving joyfully to others and receiving gratitude in return are the flow of abundance and prosperity. A perfect balance of Spirit mind and body is possible only after our own self love is in place as a strong foundation. Self love will create true happiness for us and that true happiness is on the inside, which is reflected on our outside.

Do you want to feel happy?
Do you want to feel loved?

You choose how you want to feel!

You choose what influences will control your life. You are responsible for the thoughts you allow into your mind, you are responsible for the people you associate with and you are responsible for the situations you allow yourself to be involved in.

I Love Myself!

Our Purpose is to love ourselves, to share that love with others and enjoy a life of unlimited possibilities. When we are living our

Spirit, we are living with purpose; we are naturally doing what we love and we do it with passion. When we live our true self we are sharing our gifts with those around us, our love and joy are contagious. As more and more good comes our way, those around us are affected in a positive way. Living in self love we share positive high energy vibrations, affecting those around us, which raises their energy vibration. Our positive energy connects with others inspiring them to wake up, they start feeling better and begin to feed their spirit, they in turn connect to others and the process continues to spread. As we know, we are all energetically connected. When we share our gifts with love we begin to transform our world. *We are one in ourselves, connected Spirit mind and body, and we are one as a group, connected together energetically.*

Travel the 18" from your head to your heart!

Notice how you feel right now, in this moment.

Now list 5 things you love about your life:

1. _____

2. _____

3. _____

4. _____

5. _____

Now take a moment to feel your energy. Notice: Did your energy vibration increase just thinking about the many things you love about your life? Where do you feel the energy vibration in your body?

Can you imagine if you were given the choice right now, today, to create and live the life you desire? Can you imagine what you would like your life to be? How would you present yourself in life? Would you be funny, serious, creative, a leader, a helper? How would you feel, confident, full of energy? Would you be healthy, strong with muscles toned? How would you share your gifts and talents? Are you a writer, an artist, an outstanding parent, an educator, an awesome employee? What are your talents? How do you want to contribute and be of service in the world? What is your passion?

Many of us have never 'consciously' considered what we want are lives to be. Since our behavior creates our lives, becoming more mindful and aware of what we are creating is an obvious positive choice of action. Often we consciously know what we don't want, or we focus on what we don't have, and of course the universe obliges, sending us more of what we focus on, more of what we don't want! Now that we realize we choose and create our reality when living from a place of self love we live from our heart, live our Spirit, rising up to a higher positive energy vibration we create a positive new reality, a reality we choose. We know to achieve the life we desire we change limiting beliefs and behaviors that no longer serve our highest good, this begins to dissolve our perceptions of fear. We understand the importance of taking responsibility for our negative behaviors and thoughts. We tune in, raising our awareness allowing us to change these behaviors and thoughts from negatives into positives. From a place of love we accept our emotions as loving guidance from our Spirit, our inner voice.

So let us begin this exciting journey with joyful emotions and feelings of anticipation for self discovery through the many methods available to us as we awaken our spirit and imagine the unlimited possibilities the universe is waiting to deliver to us. Let us create a higher energy vibration attracting more good into our lives as we journal with our Spirit, in gratitude, affirming the abundance that is ours for the asking. Let us intend a deeper connection with Spirit, Source, God, Universe through our daily practices of prayer, meditation and self hypnosis. Let us begin to explore with the playful intention the rediscovery of self love.

It is natural to live from our hearts in self love,

A returning home to be guided by our Spirit,

Living in harmony and balance with

The power of our mind and the strength of our body!

Phase II

Creating and Maintaining
Your New Reality
Daily Practices

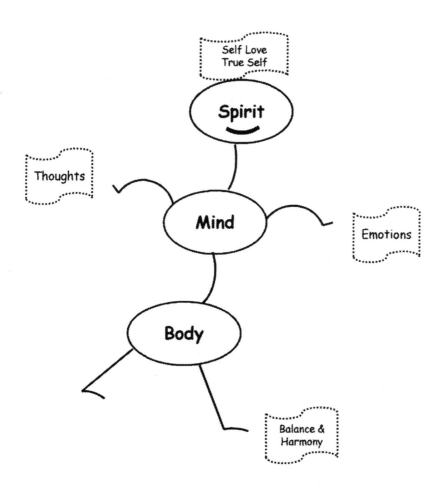

Methods and Daily Practices

The practices of awakening and connecting to your Spirit through imagination, journaling, gratitude, positive affirmations, prayer, meditation, and self hypnosis, will bring you back to Self; bring you back from living in your head where ego and fear live, to living from your heart, a place of love, the home of your Spirit. As you move back to living from your heart, living your Spirit, you develop a greater self love that will lead you toward your passion, your purpose. When you begin to live your passion you are back into the flow of your Spirit, you serve and receive in love, peace and calm, you will experience all of the abundance life has to offer. Life becomes 'easy' when you live your passion, you are in the flow, and you look forward to each day with anticipation, expecting good things to happen to you every day.

All that you seek is already inside of you,

It is all about making the connection!

There are multiple methods and daily practices available to you that will support your desire for positive change toward living your true self, loving yourself, and living your Spirit. A suggestion may be to try all of the methods for a short period of time, then after you have experience each one, pick a few that you feel comfortable with. Then develop your practices to return back to living your spirit, to living a life of passion and fulfillment.

We begin by awakening your Spirit, raising your vibration will attract more good into your life immediately!! Awakening your

Spirit is great fun because we begin to re-connect with your inner child, with the part of you that wants to have fun, be creative and play.

We then move on to learn how to further develop our imagination. The mind and our ego are powerful and helpful tools when we control them and use them to our advantage. Because the mind communicates in pictures, we use our imagination to instruct our mind in what we would like to manifest. This can be done through role playing, setting intentions with the impact of visualization and emotions to actually see and feel the outcome we desire.

A vital support method is to establish the daily practice of journaling. Journaling with your Spirit connects you with your higher self, communicating with your inner voice, your inner wisdom for guidance. Another journaling process is to journal with your inner child. Inner child journaling is a wonderful process connecting with your inner child to ask questions about behaviors, or issues you would like to resolve, but have not been able to with logic and 'willpower'. Journaling with your inner child for guidance in creativity and fun helps stay balanced with a healthy combination of work and play.

Developing the daily practice of gratitude and positive affirmations are instrumental in changing your thoughts from lack and negative self talk into positive higher vibrational energy, re-connecting with your Spirit, re-discovering, un-covering your purpose, your true life desires. We also practice effective methods to quiet your mind and communicate with your true self, with your Spirit, with Source, God, or the Universe through Prayer, Meditation and Self Hypnosis.

Daily practices will strengthen your connection to your Spirit, you become more open and receptive to following your inner guidance. When you are connected to Source, your higher energy vibration attracts more blessings into your life. When you are open you connect energetically with those around you, in connecting with others, you increase the vibration and energy of the planet.

Multiple methods and practices are available to support you in reconnecting with your Spirit, choose one or more that work best for you! Practice daily. The more you practice, the more effective you will be in opening to your Spirit, receiving guidance and acting upon it! Experiment with various combinations of methods and practices. Perhaps several different methods will work for you based on the type of guidance you are seeking.

Have fun, relax, and enjoy the process of greater, deeper self discovery!

Practice 1

Awaken Your Spirit

As we discussed earlier, true happiness comes from inside of us. External factors, possessions or persons cannot provide us with lasting happiness. External influences can enhance our experiences, enrich our lives, but only we can create true happiness for ourselves and that true happiness is on the inside, which is reflected on our outside.

> ## You Choose How You Feel!
>
> ### Do you want to feel happy?
>
> ### If the answer is "Yes!" then you must choose to awaken your spirit!

There are many ways to awaken your Spirit. You can begin right now by standing or sitting up straight, shoulders back, chest out, lift your chin up, take in a deep breath and SMILE! Did you *feel the change in your 'state'?* The words 'change in state' as used here, are similar to a status check in on the emotional temperature of your mind and body, for example after you changed your physical positioning you may have felt a little happier, a little more calm. When you make a simple change to your state for example by putting a smile on your face, you have already begun to change your mood to a happier higher energy vibration. *To awakening your Spirit you must move your body to get your energy flowing and raise your energy vibration!* Simple methods to awaken your Spirit are dance, walk, swing and sway, clap your hands, roll your shoulders, just get your body moving! Singing is another higher energy action that will awaken your spirit. Awakening your spirit is done through Self Expression, through your creative side, the inner child portion of your Spirit.

To awaken your Spirit you must raise your Spirit's energy vibration, get moving, and express your Spirit. As you awaken your Spirit you will become more aware of your body and the feelings inside your body. You will be more mindful of your energy vibration. As you raise your energy you will attract other positive energy to you, *'like attracts like', 'you get more of what you focus on'*, so as you awaken your spirit, get ready to receive more good into your life!

Ideas to Awaken Your Spirit

WAKE UP! Become conscious!! Awaken Your Spirit!

The first step toward Self Love is to make the reconnection to your Spirit. Even if you have been unconscious and your spirit is buried under a lot of dust, with just a little practice you will begin to reconnect.

Dance Practice

Check in this moment:

How do you rate your energy vibration level?

(lowest) 1 2 3 4 5 6 7 8 9 10 (highest) _____

Put on your favorite inspirational dance music to get you moving! How about music from the Disco era or hip hop, ballroom waltz or tango, or line dancing? Wake up your Spirit! Get moving, clear the area around you, stretch and get ready to move your body! Anyway your Spirit moves you! Turn on the music and just move for 5 to 10 minutes!

LIVE LARGE!

Check in now, what is your energy vibration? _____

Sing Practice

Check in this moment:

How do you rate your energy vibration level?

(lowest) 1 2 3 4 5 6 7 8 9 10 (highest) _____

Do you enjoy making a joyful noise!? What favorite song lyrics inspire you to burst into song or strengthen your resolve? Put your favorite tunes on and sing out loud, give it all you have! Stand in front of a mirror, look into your eyes, grab a hairbrush for a microphone, or better yet perhaps you have a microphone on your computer or docking station. A wonderful opportunity to burst into song is while you are driving in the car.

Sing out, or sing along, to music that inspires you, music that makes you feel happy, joyful, expresses love. Choose music that speaks to your Spirit. Open your throat Chakra, raise your vibration higher, and express yourself out loud!

LIVE OUT LOUD!

Check in now, what is your energy vibration? _____

Check In, Tune In to You, Feel Your Energy Vibration

How do you feel?

Where do you feel the energy in your body?

Do you feel your Spirit?

Has your Spirit awakened?

Are you vibrating at a higher energy level?

Feed Your Spirit through Play and Fun

When you feed your Spirit you are acknowledging your inner child. Your inner child needs play for relaxation, to feel happy, fun stirs creativity and sparks self expression.

What feeds your Spirit excites and awakens your inner child?

Would you enjoy free time to shop for or display special collectables: toys, dolls, cars, paperweights? Or perhaps fresh cut flowers in your entry, kitchen or dining room. Would it be fun to have free time to draw or paint, color with *crayolas*, or blow bubbles?

The Process of re-discovering your Spirit, your true self, begins with asking yourself questions and then 'feeling' the true answers. If your inner child has been ignored for a while, or you are not sure what is fun, or what you may like to do, write with carefree imagination, as if you were a child. For example if you could choose an activity that is fun for you and you could do it today what would you do?

If I could do anything I wanted to do right now I would . . . .

_____

_____

Now examine your answer. Close your eyes, imagine doing that activity, do you feel the happiness, joy, contentment?

When you awaken your Spirit and your Inner Child, Your Passion(s) will be made known to you; your Divine purpose will unfold.

What Makes Me Smile?

1. _____

2. _____

3. _____

4. _____

What Makes My Heart Fill with Joy?

1. _____

2. _____

3. _____

4. _____

If you could do anything you wanted to do today, anything at all, what would you want to do?

1. _____

2. _____

3. _____

What makes your heart sing, what would be fun to do today, what would feed your inner child; fill your heart with joy:

1. _____

2. _____

3. _____

Some may find these questions easy to answer, while some may find them challenging. For many of us it has been a long time since we considered what activities we love or enjoy, all too often we compromise our enjoyment choices, considering others' choices such as partners, family members or friends more important than our own. Willing and mindful compromises are a necessary part of life; however these exercises are *ALL ABOUT YOU!*

Focus on the Feeling of Fun

This next exercise helps us to wake up our inner child and focus on FUN, remember be creative, be outrageous, give no thought to expense, time or limitations in feeling your answers, feel the fun and enjoyment.

Now fill in the blanks, making a list of all the activities you find fun, creative, rewarding, or activities you would like to experience:

What do you Love to do?

1. _____   _ _ _

2. _____   _ _ _

3. _____   _ _ _

4. _____   _ _ _

5. _____   _ _ _

6. _____   _ _ _

7. _____   _ _ _

8. _____   _ _ _

9. _____   _ _ _

10. _____   _ _ _

Now please take a moment and think about the last time you did any of these activities? When is the last time you had fun?

Next we are going to take a few minutes to review and examine each activity you have listed. Doing what you love to do will strengthen your connection with your Spirit and your inner child. Feel your reaction as you imagine doing each activity. Now we reorganize the list to begin with your 'highest emotional reaction' activity which would be your most favorite activity, number ten and work down. Begin with line number one, close your eyes, imagine doing this activity, feel the reaction in your body, then open your eyes, write a number from 1–10 rating the love level of enjoyment of the activity, 10 being the highest. Do this with each line 1 through 10. If you have an internal knowing of what you love to do, scan the list and renumber 10 through 1, begin with the highest enjoyment emotion, enjoying the feeling of each activity as you proceed down the list.

This practice is multi-purpose, we remind ourselves of the things we love to do, we see how long it has been since we have had fun, and we raise our awareness of the 'feelings' we generate from the enjoyment of activities we consider fun. After you experience this practice once or twice, you will be much faster at listing what fulfills you in the area of fun, creativity and enjoyment.

This list is also a wonderful way to re-discover what may bring you fulfillment; you uncover higher purpose, or your perfect self expression. Perhaps you are considering a new career, relationship or lifestyle change; this is a great tool that will assist you in sparking your creativity and imagination, being more open to possibilities.

Suffering is optional because we choose how we feel. We choose what type of experience we want to have. Choose to be happy or choose to be unhappy, the glass is either half full or half empty, but either way you get to choose.

Practice 2

Imagination

Did I create this mess? Yes, either consciously or un-consciously, you create the life you are living in today, your current reality! What your life is today is a creation of your thoughts and actions. *We are the result of our subconscious Mind.* **Great news!** By raising our awareness, we are able to consciously control our choices; we can make conscious choices to create our new desired reality any time we choose to! We have many techniques available to help us raise our awareness, our consciousness.

Your imagination creates your reality. What you imagine and you decide is true for you becomes your reality. In this reality that you create, you decide the rules in which you live by, your behavior and choices reflect these rules. As you look around and examine your life, are there a few things you would like to change?

If you can think it and believe it, you can create it!

Imagination + Visualization = Manifestation

The mind communicates in pictures so imagination and visualization are excellent practice methods to convey to your mind what you would like to manifest. *Imagination* is the creative process you use to picture your reality. *Visualization* is the process that uses imagination to picture a specific outcome. *Manifestation* is creating a desired outcome into reality. Learning how to manifest or intend your outcome to create your new reality is accomplished through the further development of your imagination. We manifest what we desire through setting an intention, focusing on this intention we use the power of our imagination, we visualize to 'see and feel' the intended outcome, lastly believe and anticipate our intention as if it has already taken place and it is on the way, releasing any stress energy tied to a specific outcome. We combine 'seeing' the desire outcome through visualization and add the power of 'feeling' with our emotions. Now we begin to actually *see* the outcome we desire in our *mind* and *feel* the outcome we desire in our *body.* This powerful practice supports us in creating our new reality. We see and feel ourselves in the role of what we desire, so we *act as if what we desire is already available to us*, believing it is on the way, the last step is to release the outcome with gratitude, anticipating with excitement but releasing any anxiety of a specific outcome, knowing the perfect outcome is on the way.

The process of releasing the outcome is similar to saying *'thank you',* and letting go of how the request will manifest, while remaining open to receive. The Universe, Spirit, God is capable of delivering much greater possibilities than we could ever imagine. When we create an intention we have the choice of either setting specific details with our limited imagination that will limit what is delivered to us, or we can intend with broad guidelines allowing the Universe, God, Spirit, with all of the un–limited possibilities available, that we cannot even begin to imagine possible, deliver to us a perfect intention fulfilled. Un-limited possibilities are usually a first choice; the only caution is to be open to receiving and recognizing the un-limited possibility when it arrives. With limited thinking and therefore limited potential in order to recognize the opportunities when they arrive, it is more important than ever to keep in the moment, be conscious, and raise your awareness in anticipation of good things coming your way!

Very often we ask for something from the Universe, God, Source and do not even recognize the gift when it arrives because we are looking for something specific. An example would be our interest in attracting a new career opportunity. Let us consider that we are seeking a career opportunity specifically in a frame shop because we enjoy the passion of art and photography. We appreciate the challenges of choosing a perfect frame in order to display the work properly. We feel that we can be excited about a position in a frame shop because we would see art and photography as we created the appropriate frame. Perhaps we have a specific company in mind, Dan's frame shop. When our gift arrives from Source, it arrives as a position with Gloria's Gallery. The gallery position involves creating the proper display for exhibits, working with artists to set up the appropriate pieces with the appropriate frames and lighting. We may not recognize our gift as the opportunity we asked for because we were focused on a frame shop position, we ignore the gift of an 'even better' opportunity to work with art and photography which is our true passion, creating more than frames, creating the entire display. The Universe delivered greater than what we could have imagined. We were not mindful in the anticipation of our intention. We then complain that our prayers are not answered or the Universe is not listening, and slip into negative energy.

Write an intention that you would like to manifest:

_____

_____

_____

Imagine (Feel), and **Visualize (**See), your intention in your mind as if it were a movie. Imagine sense and feel in your body how you feel when your intention becomes your reality. Visualize, see with clarity in your mind how you look, how those around you look. Imagine sense and feel being there in the scene of your intention becoming a reality as the movie of your intention plays and you are the star of your movie!

Believe and anticipate the perfect outcome of your intention.

Thank you in gratitude of receiving, letting go of outcome.

Stay in Awareness in anticipation of the arrival of your intention.

Process of Manifestation

- ✓ Set a desired intention
- ✓ Focus imagination and *'see'* the visualization
- ✓ *'Feel'* the emotion
- ✓ Believe and anticipate on the way
- ✓ Thank you and let go of the outcome
- ✓ Anticipate your new Desired reality

The imagination practice includes assuming a talent or a skill that we may desire or had in the past, we *feel* and *act as if* we are the person we desire, and *see* ourselves in the situation we desire. For example if an intention is to be a successful speaker, you would want to imagine yourself up on a stage, imagine how you would speak, gesture, walk and move around the stage, visualize your appearance, hear the applause when you conclude your message and feel how you would interact with the participants after the presentation. Using imagination with visualization focusing on a specific outcome is a valuable practice that is also utilized successfully to enhance sports performance and test taking.

It is a well known, accepted principle, that we *'attract more of whatever we focus on, into our lives'*, this attraction works with our energy vibration, low energy attracts low energy, high energy attracts high energy, this is the most basic of explanations as this relates to quantum physics, beyond my area of passion. To attract more of what we desire into our lives we begin with playful imagination, perhaps you may want to call on your inner child to assist with creative inspiration.

We wear many hats during our life time, many hats during a single day. How many roles do you play in a day? How many different hats do you wear? At home are you a Mom, a chef, a chauffeur, a gardener, a dog walker? In your free time are you a pianist, a poet, a dancer, a singer, a nature lover, a baker? In your work are you a healer, a speaker, a teacher, a caregiver, an administrator, a service provider? We utilize our life experience from our many hats or personas to awaken our awareness and spark our creativity.

Awareness Exercises

Who do I choose to be?

Make a list of 10 different 'personalities' or different 'hats' you wear during the day, week, or during a month. For example: During the day you may make dinner for the family, so you are the *chef*, you may be responsible for the outdoor yard maintenance so you are the *gardener*, your profession may be a grammar school teacher so you are the *teacher*.

1. _____

2. _____

3. _____

4. _____

5. _____

6. _____

7. _____

8. _____

9. _____

10. _____

Pick several personalities that you would like to playfully explore or develop further and rewrite them below. Perhaps these personalities interest you and you would like to try these activities or you enjoyed this talent in the past, but have been away from it for a while.

1. _____

2. _____

3. _____

4. _____

5. _____

Next choose three of these personalities of interest that you would like to imagine and step into right now. List the three personalities in order of importance, number 1 being the more interesting to you for now then down to number 3.

1. _____

2. _____

3. _____

Now you are going to playfully assume your first choice personality for a few minutes. This is a fun game using your imagination, just like day dreaming only with purpose. Close your eyes, choose a personality to explore, make this personality as vivid and real as possible, and feel what it would be like to be or have this talent, have your body assume the posture of this talent if you were walking, talking, or moving about. Visualize being in this personality, make the picture large, brighten the color, turn up the sound.

Check in

Write a brief statement of how you felt *'Being'* each of these preferred personalities? Were you comfortable? Did you feel joy or happiness? How do you feel now? Where do you feel the energy in your body? Do you feel your Spirit, is it awake? Are you vibrating at a higher energy level?

1. _____

_____

_____

2. _____

_____

_____

3. _____

_____

_____

This is a wonderful exercise to 'remember' enjoyable activities you have forgotten or to discover new, fun interests. A point here is to go back to your original list of the 10 personalities. Are there any functions on this list that you no longer enjoy? If any personalities no longer serve your highest good, is it possible to eliminate these functions or reduce the time spent in them to allow for the further development of a new interest, an interest that may be more fun, add more joy into your life?

Vision Boards

Creating your own personal vision board is a fun and happy project. There are no rules. You choose what you want to focus on, your career, a new home, travel, whatever you want to manifest into your life. Once you decide what you want to manifest, take a few days or weeks to collect pictures, words, maybe even small symbols or items that will represent what your intention is. The idea is to create the board(s) to remind you of your intentions. They are a visual representation of your desire which will support your imagination in attracting what you intend to manifest into your life every time you pass by and look at them. The more often you see the vision boards, the more often you are reminded of your intentions. The images help create the feelings that will add power to the imagined and visualized intention.

When you have collected all of your meaningful pieces set aside some quiet personal time. Creating your vision board is a time to relax and have fun. You are creating a visual of what you intend to manifest. Enjoy the process as you mount the images, words and any small items you have collected onto a piece of poster board, foam board, art paper or even a large roll of paper. Vision boards are private; there is no need for explanation to anyone unless you feel the need to share. Keep in mind that although well meaning, others may easily dash dreams and aspirations simply with a single word or expression. Perhaps this is too fragile of a time to receive solicited or un-solicited input from well intentioned onlookers. Vision boards are heartfelt; they are your creation as a reflection of your desires. The private space available to you will most likely dictate the type of materials you use.

Materials needed: scissors, glue stick, magazines to cut images and words from, poster board or heavy roll paper, or heavy art paper. Imagination!

Have Fun!

Practice 3

Journaling

Journaling is recognized as an 'insightful' daily practice by many different professions. Journaling is a proven, successful technique when applied in spiritual practice, professional therapy, medical recovery therapy, and weight management programs. Journaling brings your thoughts, beliefs and behavior into your awareness, as you become more mindful, your ability to make positive choices increases. The purpose of journaling is to connect with your inner self, your thoughts, your emotions, your beliefs, your subconscious mind, your creativity and your inner wisdom. Journaling is a very powerful tool, whether you are journaling your thoughts and feelings, or connecting with your Spirit or connecting with your inner child.

In my private practice, I have observed that some clients express hesitation, an underlying fear, of the journaling process. The initial opposition to the journaling process is the excuse of the lack of time available each day; to set aside thirty minutes receives resistance. However, I believe that often the hesitation to journal is more a concern of what may be revealed once written down. A perception is that it is too painful to acknowledge what will be written down, no longer deniable once written and out in the open. The good news about statements or thoughts that are out in the open into awareness and written down, is that you can examine the statement(s) and ask, "Is this true for me?

Do I really believe this now or is it just an old action or thought that is more of a habit, an unconscious thought?"

Writing adds power to a thought, emotion, or idea, writing is *second only to speaking* the words of a thought, emotion or idea. Once we add power to our thoughts with words, speaking or writing them, we then see this thought, emotion or idea, as the 'truth' for us. Our words, thoughts, emotions when spoken have an undeniable power, and they cannot be taken back, once in the open out of the bottle so to speak, they must be dealt with. This can cause great fear because we may not want to reveal this part of us, in fear we may feel that these thoughts will make us even more un-lovable, un-worthy. And once written, we fear that we will like ourselves even less! The fear of revealing more of ourselves and having to face what we believe is our truth is understandable. *The great news is that it is not the 'truth'; once again it is our perception of the truth and easily changed!* However we cannot change what we are unwilling to acknowledge.

The daily practice of thirty minutes of journaling will surprise you with 'Aha' ideas, inspiration and answers to questions you have may have been pondering. It is fun and rewarding to be in contact with the real you. The only necessary materials are a pen and notebook, a simple spiral bound or an elegant leather bound journal, you choose what works best for you. My personal journaling style is a special purple pen to write with and inexpensive wide rule lined spiral notebooks with colorful, playful covers.

The journaling process, with either your Spirit or your Inner Child, is a vital, necessary, support practice when you are in the process of re-discovering self love and your true

authentic Spirit. I cannot stress this enough. I appreciate with our busy lives it may be challenging to schedule thirty minutes for journaling first thing in the morning before your day starts. Please trust me, this is time very well spent, should you decide to incorporate this into your routine, the returns on this practice are multiplied exponentially. I highly recommend the daily practice of journaling, with your Spirit and/or your inner child, be established during the first few months of developing your new routines for your desired changes.

In general the practice of journaling is also valuable and very supportive when following the daily practice of prayer or meditation. Journaling is a wonderful opportunity to write down the guidance you receive from your connection to Spirit. When you become more comfortable with the changes in your life, perhaps you may choose to cut back on your time spent journaling, it is up to you to decide what works best for you. *Some discontinue journaling because all is going well in their life, others continue to journal because all is going well in their life.*

Journaling with Your Spirit

Journaling with your Spirit connects you with your higher self, communicating with your inner voice, your inner wisdom for guidance.

Journaling with your Spirit for guidance is very effective in uncovering what may be blocking you from achieving your new desired behavior. When you journal with your Spirit you receive insight into new creative ideas, or solutions to issues, you experience 'Aha' moments.

First thing every morning, before the day begins, as you sit in the silence, just begin to write whatever comes to mind for about thirty minutes or three notebook pages. Often the first few minutes of journaling are more like a 'to do list' for the day, but after a few minutes ideas start to flow, dialog brings ideas to the surface, creativity opens up. When I am seeking guidance I write a question that reflects my issue. For example, if I am questioning my purpose, I may ask, "What is mine to do?" The benefit of writing out your thoughts and concerns is that writing adds more power to your thoughts. If you speak out loud as you write, you enhance the positive energy even more. When you write a negative thought, quickly reverse it and re-write the positive, speaking the positive out loud. Your thoughts and ideas that surface are guidance from your Spirit, you will receive solutions, inspiration, sparks of creativity, moments of awakening.

Connect with your Inner Child

Inner child journaling is a wonderful tool that will help you to connect with your inner child. Journaling exercises with your inner child offer great insight to your emotions and to your blocking behaviors. Use the journaling process to ask questions about your undesired behaviors. You may also journal about issues you would like to resolve, but have not been able to with logic and 'willpower'. Inner child journaling is a very effective technique when used for re-discovery and guidance helpful in sparking your creativity and fun. Actively pursuing creativity and fun will help you stay balanced by enjoying a healthy combination of both work and play.

Journaling with Your Inner Child Writing Exercise

Inner child journaling connects you with your inner child. With this connection you ask questions about specific behaviors or issues you would like to resolve, ask questions that assist in re-igniting creativity, questions that help you connect with your passion. Your inner child can help you put 'fun' back into your life.

In your journal notebook write a question you would like to ask your inner child. Then close your eyes, relax and imagine how your inner child would respond, sit in quiet for a few moments, then open your eyes and begin writing your inner child's response into your notebook.

An example of a question for your inner child might be, "If you could do anything right now that was fun for you, what would it be?" When your subconscious answers a question the answer is 'the truth for you', whether or not it is a fact, what matters is that it is 'true for you' in your reality. The reply from your inner child is a connection with a part of your Spirit.

As you practice you may choose to ask deeper questions of your inner child that will uncover limiting beliefs and behaviors that you would like to change. As we discussed earlier, all beliefs and behaviors were originally formed in our subconscious to protect us. Now that these beliefs no longer serve our highest good, we need to ask our subconscious what purpose the limiting belief served. Then we need to ask what would be a healthy replacement that would still protect us, but support us in a more positive way.

Continue this practice as needed to stay in touch with your inner child, uncovering hidden emotions and staying focused on resolving any issues that limit you. This written dialog between your adult self and your inner child will reveal issues held on a deeper level. Reply to your adult self questions from a child's perspective, your inner child's eyes. What would be fun to do? If you could do anything, what would it be? How would you feel? How would you look? What inspires you? Once you are aware of your limiting thoughts and beliefs, aware of the type of fun you desire to make yourself happier, you will be able to make the appropriate changes in your behavior to satisfy your inner child, this in turn will help you to be more satisfied with you and your life! Journaling daily is recommended, as it keeps you in touch with yourself. Another benefit is that it is always a pleasant surprise when creative ideas and solutions to what was keeping you stuck pop out as you write or shortly afterward when you least expect it. Journaling is a very creative way to keep in touch with your True Spirit on a daily basis.

Inner Child Journaling Sample Questions

Questions to inspire fun, play and creativity:

What makes your heart sing?

What makes you smile?

What do you love to do?

What would you enjoy doing today?

What would you do if you could do anything you wanted to do today?

When you take time to appreciate and love yourself, you realize that 'play' is an important part of being centered and joyful. Take time out at least once a day to do one activity that will make you feel great, an ice cream cone, a few minutes in the park, a few minutes reading a good book, taking the dog for a walk.

Questions to make a connection with a limiting belief or behavior, unexpressed emotions, relationship issues:

Why are you so angry?

Why do you feel sad?

What are you afraid of?

Why do you get so nervous?

Why does he (she) irritate you so much?

The purpose of these questions is to bring the 'feeling' forward into your awareness. As we discussed earlier, once you are aware of the feeling, you are then able to acknowledge it and move on. Many of us are afraid of our emotions, so we do not express them, *the fact is the real fear of emotions is not having them; it is having them and not releasing them, or feeling them.* We mentioned earlier that emotions are like waves on the ocean, they come and go. Emotions have energy; this energy must be felt and expressed for health reasons. Un-expressed emotions are unexpressed energy. This un-expressed energy is trapped in your body. Un-expressed emotions create energy blocks, when energy is trapped in your body the results are serious health risks. Un-expressed emotions can manifest as a serious illness, cancer, heart disease, high blood pressure, chronic pain, and chronic fatigue just to name a few.

Journaling is a revealing and healing therapy, this daily practice is a supportive tool that only requires your time and a simple spiral bound notebook. Who better to provide the answers you seek than yourself? Who knows you better than you? Trusting in you is trust well placed!

Practice 4

The Power of Daily Gratitude, Self Love and Appreciation

Daily Gratitude, Self Love, and Appreciation are joyful practices that when used daily, deepen your connection to your Spirit, God, Source, to the Universe, and those around you. Daily gratitude, self love and appreciation also create a *happier you*. By following the practice of reflecting on all the good you currently have in your life you will feel happier. The practice of gratitude reminds us how fortunate and blessed we truly are. Often we only see our glass as half empty, wanting more, or feeling like there is not enough, instead of seeing the abundance in our lives and all the prosperity held in the half full glass. When we change our thoughts from lack, seeing only what is missing from our lives, to appreciation and gratitude for what we have, we raise ourselves to a higher vibrational energy. We begin to re-connect with our Spirit, re-discover, and un-cover our purpose, our true life desires.

The journey from your head back to your heart begins when you raise your awareness and connect with your feelings. Awareness begins with paying attention to your thoughts and your emotions. Gratitude is a wonderful way to instantly help you feel happier, appreciate all that you have and raise your energy to a higher vibration, ultimately attracting more good into your life. Developing a greater awareness of your feelings and the ability to change your state to a greater level of happiness begins by answering these three statements as a daily practice, *"Today I am grateful for, What I love about me today is, What I appreciate in my life today is "*.

Before we begin this exercise, please take a moment to check in with yourself. Close your eyes down, scan your body, how do you feel? If you were to rate an overall number from 1 to 10, 10 being a really great feeling of happiness or contentment, where would you rate yourself right now?

Write that number here _____

Take a few moments to fill out the following statements. Begin with the first section "Today, I am grateful for".

Today, I Am Grateful for:

1. _____

2. _____

3. _____

4. _____

5. _____

6. _____

After you have filled in the six lines, close your eyes down for a moment and check in with your emotions, how do you feel right now? Rate your feeling of happiness or contentment now. Number from 1 to 10, 10 being a really great feeling of happiness or contentment, where would you rate yourself right now?

Write that number here _____

Take a few moments to fill out the following statement "What I love about me today is".

What I Love About Me Today is:

1. _____

2. _____

3. _____

4. _____

5. _____

6. _____

After you have filled in the six lines, close your eyes down for a moment and check in with your emotions, how do you feel right now? Rate your feeling of happiness or contentment now. Number from 1 to 10, 10 being a really great feeling of happiness or contentment, where would you rate yourself right now?

Write that number here _____

Take a few moments to fill out the following statement "What I appreciate in my life today is".

What I Appreciate in My Life Today is:

1. _____

2. _____

3. _____

4. _____

5. _____

6. _____

After you have filled in the six lines, close your eyes down for a moment and check in with your emotions, how do you feel right now? Rate your feeling of happiness or contentment now. Number from 1 to 10, 10 being a really great feeling of happiness or contentment, where would you rate yourself right now?

Write that number here _____

The purpose of this exercise is to demonstrate how *'thinking'* about all of the things we have to be grateful for, *'thinking'* about all of the things we love about ourselves and *'thinking'* about what we appreciate in our lives *'physically'* effects us, we feel better physically, we feel happier because of our positive high energy thoughts.

Thoughts + Emotion = Body reaction

How do your numbers look? Did you start out at a lower number, a lower rate of happiness or contentment, and then with each exercise, gradually begin to feel a higher level of happiness, increasing your rating? Did you feel an increase in positive energy as you filled in each line? Did your numbers go up with each exercise? Can you feel the difference in your happiness or contentment level right now after completing this exercise? Can you feel a higher energy vibration right now? The benefits of gratitude, self love and appreciation affect us emotionally and physically. It is important for us to know that we can change how we feel in any given moment. *Anytime we choose to we can change our thoughts to happiness and contentment simply by taking a moment to mentally list what we are grateful for in this present moment of awareness.*

Today, I Am Grateful for: Day: _____

1. _____

2. _____

3. _____

4. _____

What I Love About Me Today is:

1. _____

2. _____

3. _____

4. _____

What I Appreciate in My Life Today is:

1. _____

2. _____

3. _____

4. _____

Practice 5

Positive Affirmations

A positive affirmation is a brief statement, a sentence or two, which is stated in the present tense, composed using a positive choice of words that express a desire or intention you want to manifest or focus on. The positive affirmation is repeated as often as possible during the day. The phrase or phrases maybe written on index cards or 'post its', or on your smart phone, wherever on whatever medium works best for you, the objective is to see and read your affirmations throughout the day.

Positive affirmations are reminders of what we want to manifest into our lives. They are thoughts that we want to focus on that will create the feelings we desire, this then creates positive energy and attracts more of what we desire into our life. Affirmations also replace any negative thoughts, or negative behaviors, or negative self talk we want to change. For example:

"Each and every day, more good things come my way"

"I choose to let go of what was and I live what is"

"Money Flows easily in unexpected ways into My Life"

"In Spirit Mind and Body I Am Whole and Well"

During a lapse of awareness positive affirmations will change a negative thought that may have slipped into your mind. It will change your energy to a higher vibration to attract more good into your life. Positive affirmations are similar to standing up straight, shoulders back and putting a smile on your face, they will change your 'state' of mind from negative to positive, from worried to calm, they are uplifting. Positive affirmations are an excellent tool to use in addition to your daily practices of prayer, meditation and self hypnosis. Therapeutic Suggestions used in self hypnosis are very similar to positive affirmations and in some cases they may be the same. Unity teaches a technique of 'Denials and affirmations', to acknowledge an issue, behavior or habit, make the statement to deny it has power over you, and then state the positive you wish to intend. In this process you acknowledge the issue that you want to overcome or change, *"My feelings of unworthiness"*, state it has no power over you, *"have no power over me"*, then state the positive, *"I am talented, loved and special "*. An example of a denial with a positive affirmation statement would be: My feelings of unworthiness have no power over me; I am talented, loved, and special.

Repetition is key to support any lasting change; the same is true in the use of positive affirmations. Write your affirmations on cards or 'post its'. Place them in private areas so you we see them throughout the day, read and speak affirmations out loud as many times as possible. You may choose to compose several, four to six, if so change them up and write new ones whenever you feel the need, keeping them fresh keeps your interest and emotional energy at a higher vibrational level. Always state your affirmations in the positive, present tense with feeling. If the present tense is not 'believable' then use ***more and more every day and in every way'***, this helps the subconscious believe with emotion that the affirmation is true. Remember, saying your affirmations with emotion will add more power to your words and intentions. Declaring your affirmations with emotion and imagination, feeling and seeing, then believing what you are saying creates the highest energy possible. The higher your energy, the more you are attracting and manifesting what you truly desire. The final step in creating and manifesting, is to give thanks, believing your desire is on its way.

The subconscious mind cannot distinguish fact from fiction so positive affirmations are a powerful tool when replacing negative thoughts and limiting beliefs.

The mind does not recognize NO or NOT, so when you create an affirmation avoid those words. For example, If you say "I am not tired" your mind hears "I am Tired", the proper wording is to state the positive, "I am energized".

Sample Affirmations

Feel free to use or change these examples or create your own. Often rhymes are easy to remember and fun to say.

I release all negative thoughts and feelings that hold me back from being my highest and best self

I create my own reality

I choose to love and accept myself unconditionally at all times

I appreciate myself and treat myself with respect

I speak from my heart; I speak from a place of Love

I am a joyful and creative spirit

My awareness grows, as my good flows

Life always offers me opportunities to grow and learn

Money flows easily into my life

My perfect work is rewarded with perfect pay

In energy and flow, I give lovingly and receive joyfully

If you are seeking further inspiration, additional resources for positive affirmations can be found in some of the books listed in additional suggested reading at the back of this book. Perhaps a few sources that you may find helpful specifically for affirmations are: *How to Create an Exceptional Life*, by Louise Hay and Cheryl Richardson, *The New Game of Life*, by Ruth L. Miller, *This Thing Called You*, by Ernest Holmes, and the *Daily Word*, a Unity publication.

<u>Sample Positive Affirmation Format</u>

More and more every day . . . .

1.

2.

3.

More and more every day, and in every way . . . .

1.

2.

3.

Every day in more ways I am . . . .

1.

2.

3.

Practice 6

Prayer

The intention of this book is spiritually based on the acknowledgement of a Source greater that ourselves. What you choose to call this Source as stated earlier is your choice, Spirit, God, Universe, Source, All that Is, Mother Earth.

The process and benefits of Prayer must be addressed because prayer is a valuable daily practice to connect with Your Spirit. The word 'Prayer' has many different interpretations and perceptions. For our purposes the definition of *'Prayer'* is to *quiet the mind and connect to your Source*. When we quiet the mind we become more open, allowing for a direct communication with Source, with our Spirit, God, with our inner wisdom. This description of Prayer is similar to meditation, the purpose of both is to quiet the mind, connect, listen, and receive guidance.

There are as many methods of prayer as there are people who pray. For myself I usually start my day with ten to forty minutes or either prayer or meditation, based on how I feel that morning and my schedule. You may find that five to ten minutes works for you with several five to ten minute prayer breaks during the day. Some may choose to pray while taking a walk out of doors in nature. I follow my prayer and meditation with journaling to make note of the guidance that came through to me. For me personally I find first thing in the morning before the day begins is best for consistency in my daily practices routine.

There are many 'styles' of prayer, some choose to wear special prayer shawls, position themselves close to an alter, or space containing inspirational items, or burn incense. There are also many different positions for your body during the practice of prayer. There is not a right or wrong style of prayer. What works best for you is always the best approach to consider in all areas of your life. For quiet prayer you might sit in a chair, sit crossed legged on the floor, lie on a bed, lie on the floor, kneel, or kneel with forehead close to the floor, choose a position that is comfortable for you. Once comfortable, we then quiet the mind, letting thoughts float by, we focus on being quiet. You may choose to focus on your breath when you first enter the silence as it helps to quiet the mind. When we pray we may receive guidance that may come to us in the form of an idea, or as an image, or we may hear our inner voice. We might pray asking for something to occur; perhaps we pray to give thanks for what we have been given and for what we have received. We may feel the need to plead in desperation, or shout in anger, or cry in sadness, or we may choose to pray for others, known or unknown to us. *There is not a particular style or technique that is the correct or proper way to pray. The purpose of prayer is to be comfortable, quiet our mind and connect to our Source.* When we are open and connected we raise our energy vibration. When we pray we are open to attract more good into our lives. We are open for guidance and gifts to be presented to us, mindful in anticipation ready to accept and acknowledge them. With the daily practice of prayer we strengthen our connection to our source. When we feel connected, we feel safe, calm at peace. So when we begin to feel stress or anxiety, a technique to re-center ourselves may be to practice prayer, 5 or 10 minutes, throughout our day. Again the effects of Prayer are similar to meditation. Practicing meditation 5 or 10 minutes throughout the day will also relieve any stress or tension so that you remain calm, relaxed and centered though the day.

We discuss both prayer and meditation because they offer similar benefits in the spiritual, emotional, and physical effects they have on our Spirit, Mind and Body. The Spirit, Mind Body connection is essential for us to be in health and balance. They both accomplish the balanced Spirit, Mind Body connection quickly, easily and efficiently. Prayer and meditation are available to you anytime you choose whenever you feel the desire; there is no cost, no special preparation, and you will experience the benefits of improved health with less stress, feeling better, mentally and physically.

Sample Prayers

Feel free to use or change these samples. You may find it very meaningful to sit quietly and create your own heartfelt dialog to serve the purpose of your prayer.

Financial Abundance

Dear _____ (God, Spirit, Universe, All that Is)

Thank you for all that I have, as I give joyfully, I receive with gratitude, Thank you, Amen

Dear _____ (God, Spirit, Universe, All that Is)

I surrender to you, I let go of all thoughts of lack and limitation. By your grace I ask to live in your abundance as all my needs are provided for in a perfect way. I receive in gratitude, as I give joyfully; there is always more than enough. Thank you for all that I have. Amen

Health

Dear _____ (God, Spirit, Universe, All that Is)

I surrender all my concerns to you knowing that perfect health is mine. As I breathe in health and love I breathe out any worries or fear. I am centered and calm knowing I am a perfect child of the universe, loved and connected. Thank you for my perfect health, All is as it should be, Amen.

Dear _____ (God, Spirit, Universe, All that Is)

Thank you for my healthy body, for all the health and vitality that flows through me now, strengthening every part of me as I renew healthy in Spirit Mind and Body, Thank you, And so it is, Amen

Pray for Others

Dear _____ (God, Spirit, Universe, All that Is)

Thank you for all of my blessings. I ask that those in need of love and support feel your love and connection in the best way possible so they may be at peace in mind and relaxed in body, their Spirit full of grace.

Dear _____ (God, Spirit, Universe, All that Is)

For all of those in need of calm, peace, support, and love, I pray for them the perfect outcome, Thy will be done, Amen

Purpose

Dear _____ (God, Spirit, Universe, All that Is)

Please guide me toward my perfect self expression. Please show me the perfect way to use my many talents. I am open and ready to receive guidance. Thank you, Amen.

Dear _____ (God, Spirit, Universe, All that Is)

Please reveal to me what is mine to do. Thank you, Amen

Relationship

Dear _____ (God, Spirit, Universe, All that Is)

I am open and ready to receive the perfect relationship in a perfect way. I ask that I attract the perfect partner to share in all of the love and joy that is available through you. I surrender all fears and false limitations knowing that I am a perfect expression of myself. Thank you, And so it is.

Dear _____ (God, Spirit, Universe, All that Is)

Thank you for all those I love and for all of those who love me. Thank you for bringing the perfect partner into my life at the perfect time. Thank you, and so it is. Amen

Thank you Prayers

Dear _____ (God, Spirit, Universe, All that Is)

Thank you for all that I Am. Thank you for all that I have. I am open to joyfully give my perfect self expression in Service. Please use me for my best and highest good. Thank you, Amen

Dear _____ (God, Spirit, Universe, All that Is)

Thank you God, Thank you Spirit, for all of my Blessings. Thank you Source for all you have given me today and for my Blessings to come. Amen

---

This is a very favorite of mine!

Thank You, Thank you, Thank you,

for all that I am, for all that I have, Alleluia!

There are many wonderful, inspiritational resources for further Prayer examples. Many can be found in the additional suggested reading pages in the back of this book. Several books that may be of specific interest are; *This Thing Called You*, Ernest Holms, The New Game of Life and How to Play It, original text by Florence Scovel Shinn, edited by Ruth L. Miller, *Daily Word*, Unity Publication, *Return to Love*, by Marianne Williamson, *Law of Divine Compensation* by Marianne Williamson

Practice 7

Meditation

The overall purpose of meditation is to quiet your Mind and connect with your Spirit, your inner voice, God, Source, All that Is. Meditation is a wonderful tool to re-energize during the day or to relieve stress throughout your day. Meditation is also a very valuable tool when you are stuck or unable to make a decision. Meditation is very effective when seeking answers or direction in your life. When you choose to ask a question or seek guidance on a particular issue, the process would be to quiet your mind, ask the question, focus on your breathing, listen, receive the guidance, and then act on the message you received. During this process of quieting your mind there are many secondary benefits. For example:

Meditation Benefits Your Spirit by quieting your mind. A quiet mind allows you to be open to receive guidance, you are open to listen to your inner wisdom, and you are able to hear the message being given to you. During meditation when your mind is quiet, you are open to connect with your Spirit, when you are connected with your Spirit you are open to communicate with source. When your mind is quiet you raise your vibration to connect with others.

Meditation Benefits Your Mind with quiet. When your mind is quiet you are at peace. You feel centered throughout the day. A quiet mind is more available to hear your inner voice. A quiet mind is open and receptive, generating a higher energy vibration which attracts more good into your life.

Meditation Benefits Your Body with calm balance. When your body is relaxed and calm, your body is in healthy balance, restoring and renewing itself. The medical benefits include relieving stress and deep healthy breathing that re-oxygenates the blood.

Meditation Techniques

When practicing meditation, there are many styles and techniques to choose from. You may choose to listen to a 'guided' meditation; this is when you listen to a pre-recorded meditation, often with a stated purpose or pre-determined focus. More often you may choose to just quiet your mind on your own, with or without asking a question for guidance. As in prayer there is not a right or wrong way to meditate. Create a style of your own, one that you are comfortable with. The more comfortable you are with finding what works best for you; the more likely you are to practice. The more you practice the faster you will achieve your desired results and benefits. The purpose of meditation is to quiet your mind allowing connection with your Spirit and Source. For myself, first thing in the morning works best for about thirty to forty minutes of guided meditation when I am seeking specific answers or guidance. Some may find that ten minutes of quite meditation several times during the day works well. At times you may find playing appropriate music in the background an enjoyable experience while meditating. To begin meditation make yourself comfortable in a chair, or on the floor, turn off all electronics, phones, computers, and an idea may be, if you are in a busy household, perhaps a 'Do Not Disturb' sign on the door. Once you are comfortable, in a quiet space, begin to focus on your breathing; this begins to slow your mind and body down. Take in a few nice long inhales, filling up your lungs completely, followed by long slow exhales, then breathe normally. As you focus on your breathing you reduce stress, as you focus on your breath, you connect with your Spirit; at this point you relax into the silence, or if you choose to ask for guidance, relax and listen to your inner voice.

Sample Guided Meditations

Free Meditation Download on Website Code 'LOVE'

Short Guided Meditation to
Re-Center and De-Stress During the Day

Meditation to Re–Center yourself during a stressful day or during a stressful situation is very calming. By returning you to your breath even for five or ten minutes you return to a feeling of balance.

As you enter into this silence . . . . to center yourself . . . . back into this present moment . . . set aside the cares of the day . . . letting go of what has already occurred . . . letting go of what is to come . . . make your body comfortable . . . in your chair . . . or on the floor . . . close your eyes down and turn inward. Take in a nice long, deep inhale . . . in through your nose . . . and gently . . . let out an even longer . . . . full exhale . . .

Good . . . again . . . let's take in another nice long breath . . . breathing in through the noise . . . and exhale gently . . . letting go of any tension held anywhere in your body.

Take these few breaths to stop and re-center back into this moment. Now focus on your breath. As you sit quietly and listen to your breathing . . . letting go of any thoughts that may arise . . . . just let them float by . . . untouched vanishing in to the distance. As you breathe in . . . sit in the silence of knowing that all things are possible. As you breathe out . . . exhale any doubts or worry. As you breathe in . . . feel and know in this present moment . . . you are supported and loved . . . As you breathe out . . . exhale saying the word 'peace' . . . As you take in your next breath . . . breathing in peace . . . relax into the silence knowing you are here for a greater purpose . . . you are here to share your gifts and talents . . . to live your life in Peace . . . Happiness . . . Love . . . and Joy . . . connected to your higher wisdom and source. As you breathe out . . . breathe out any tension that remains in your body . . . letting go of all thoughts and concerns. Relax . . . rest . . . feel at peace . . . with all of creation.

Sit in the silence . . . aware of your breath . . . breathe gently . . . and just be aware of this moment . . . be present . . . aware of your breath . . . sit and enjoy the connection to your inner wisdom . . . Source . . . **rest here in this silence for a few minutes** *. . . .*

At this point, you choose, 5-10 minutes to rest in the silence

And now . . . as you begin to slowly turn your awareness back into the room . . . take your time . . . whenever you are ready to return . . . feel the peace . . . . feel the contentment of this moment. Breathing in fill up your lungs . . . breathe in deeply . . . feeling the love . . . the support of Spirit, the Universe, Source . . . feel the calm, as you return . . . connected, safe and relaxed. As you slowly exhale . . . when you are ready . . . open your eyes . . . coming back to this present moment . . . ready to experience a greater connection to your Spirit, to Source, to your Inner Wisdom.

You are ready to return to your day . . . . feeling relaxed . . . centered . . . and energized.

Guided Meditation to Restore Energy and Relax

Meditation to Restore energy and relax your Spirit, mind and body is a wonderful tool whether first thing in the morning, at the end of your day or in the middle of your day. As you sit in the silence and quiet your mind you expand your energy to the farthest edges and return calm, restored and at peace.

*Now I invite you to make yourself comfortable . . . in whatever way possible . . . . in your chair, arms relaxed, feet flat on the floor . . . . or perhaps on the floor . . . sitting or lying down . . . . Your arms relaxed, legs uncrossed. And then if you would . . . . take in a nice gentle, deep breath . . . . in through your nose . . . filling up your lungs . . . . and as you exhale . . . and **just gently close your eyes down** . . . . Letting go of any concerns, any past or future thoughts or concerns . . . . Just relax into this moment.*

Again . . . . Take in a nice deep breath . . . . breathing in peace . . . . filling up your lungs . . . hold for a moment or two . . . . then a long exhale . . . . releasing any remaining stress or tension held anywhere in your body or in your mind . . . . And say to you self the word 'peace'.

Now just breathe normally . . . a gentle . . . rhythmic breath . . . . in through your nose . . . . out through slightly parted lips . . . . Focusing on your breath . . . .

Now as you relax . . . safe . . . comfortable . . . and at peace . . . . imagine sense . . . and feel . . . . a beautiful beam of white light . . . . coming down from above . . . . perhaps a Divine . . .

healing light . . . and warm energy . . . . Of God . . . of Source . . . of Spirit . . . . descending down upon you from above . . . . to your crown chakra . . . . At the top of your head. Imagine . . . this beautiful white light of relaxing . . . healing . . . energy . . . flowing down from above . . . .

Imagine . . . sense . . . and feel the warm . . . relaxing . . . . Healing energy moving down now into your chest . . . . down through your back . . . . Warm . . . relaxing energy . . . Moving into all the back muscles . . . . the back muscles becoming loose . . . and limp . . . and relaxed. Send the warm . . . healing energy . . . . down into your hips and legs . . . . warm . . . relaxing . . . energy flows down into your knees and calves . . . . send the warm . . . relaxing . . . energy down into your ankles . . . . and feet . . . . relaxing energy flows all the way down into your feet . . . can you imagine white light energy . . . radiates out through your toes. Breathe . . .

Imagine . . . . Healing . . . white light . . . energy radiating now . . . . all though your body . . . . and can you imagine . . . healing energy . . . . Filling your mind with peace . . . . and calm . . . imagine . . . sense and feel . . . . the warm . . . relaxing light . . . . expanding the edges of your energy body . . . . can you imagine . . . . your light energy . . . radiating out . . . . Further . . . and further . . . . expanding the edges of your energy . . . . More and more . . . . Imagine this energy connecting you with God . . . with Source . . . . with Spirit . . . . With the earth . . . . and all of creation . . . . as you rest here . . . . feeling safe . . . . And completely at peace . . . breathe . . . .

Perhaps as you rest here . . . . Safe . . . and comfortable . . . . Radiating beautiful white light . . . imagine . . . . expanding your energy edges . . . further and further . . . you may choose to drift along . . . floating on a puffy . . . . white cloud . . . . resting in the mist . . . . the expansive turquoise . . . . Blue sky above . . . or perhaps you are lying comfortably in a meadow . . . . On a soft carpet of green grass . . . . as the scent of fresh mown lawn drifts by . . . . Or perhaps you are floating along . . . . In a calm . . . . Gently flowing river . . . . The refreshing sound of water softly bubbling . . . the clear sparkling water . . . . Gently cascading . . . over the shallow rocks. Rest here . . . safe . . . comfortable . . . **breathe** *. . . . feel the energy . . . restore . . . . refresh*

As you gently breathe in . . . . you feel at peace . . . relaxed . . . calm flowing all through your body and mind . . . feel the warm . . . relaxing . . . . healing energy . . . . Restoring . . . . And energizing . . . . every cell . . . every nerve . . . . all through your body and mind . . . . As you drift and float . . . . Float and drift . . . . relaxed and comfortable . . . any thoughts that may arise . . . . Just continue to drift by . . . . **Breathe** *. . . Your body . . . . and your mind . . . relax . . . . restore . . . . And rest . . . . as a divine white light radiates all though your body . . . all through your mind . . . . You feel at peace . . . . Calm . . . . connected . . . Rest here for a moment as you enjoy being at one with God, Source, Spirit, earth, and all of creation . . . .*

At this point you may sit in silence for as long as you desire

This Divine energy is available to you anytime you choose to relax, re-store, or re center yourself . . . . Just close your eyes down . . . . gently breathe in . . . . A long inhale through your nose . . . . an even longer . . . . gentle exhale . . . . out through slightly parted lips . . . . releasing any stress . . . . or tension . . . .

as you exhale . . . . Say to yourself the word . . . 'Peace' . . . . Repeat this process three times . . . . To re center . . . refresh . . . and relax every part of you.

And now that your body and mind are rested . . . . relaxed . . . and refreshed . . . . Gently . . . begin to pull your energy back . . . back into your body and mind . . . . And when you are ready . . . . Begin to wiggle your toes . . . . and wiggle your fingers tips . . . . Your awareness . . . begins to return to the room . . . . and to your surroundings . . . . As you gradually become aware of your body . . . . Your mind remains peaceful and calm . . . . Aware of your steady . . . deep . . . calming . . . breath . . . you feel centered . . . . connected to God, Source, Spirit . . . . Gently . . . . When you are ready . . . open your eyes. You are ready to return to your day . . . . feeling relaxed . . . refreshed . . . energized . . . restored. Welcome back!

You are ready to return to your day . . . . feeling relaxed . . . centered . . . and energized.

Practice 8

Hypnotherapy

The term '*Hypnotherapy*' for our purposes will be interchangeable with the terms '*Hypnosis*' and '*self hypnosis*' however just a quick note on the technical difference between the terms. *Hypnotherapy* is the industry term to describe one who practices hypnosis and who also possesses a deeper knowledge, additional study hours and skill level, specifically in the medical application of hypnosis. For example in my private practice I work with clients to reduce their level of chronic pain, reduce or eliminate cancer treatment side effects, relaxation techniques for migraines, stress and anxiety. The application and uses of *Hypnosis* may apply to improved study and sports performance, stop smoking and weight management sessions, or an entertainment performance on stage with willing participants. *Self hypnosis* is the application of self guided practice using hypnosis to change undesired behaviors and thoughts using proven hypnosis techniques. Hypnotherapy, Hypnosis and self hypnosis are all very effective methods in accomplishing positive change though 're-programming' your subconscious mind. With hypnosis and strong emotional desire you will experience immediate positive change in behavior, perceptions and limiting beliefs. On the journey back to the Heart, in the development of greater self love, the primary obstacles are usually limiting beliefs such as of low self esteem, unworthiness, lack of connection to others. Many find hypnosis a more rapid method in accomplishing desired results. Hypnosis accesses the subconscious more rapidly than prayer and meditation.

"Why is hypnosis so effective in so many areas and applications?" Hypnotherapy, hypnosis, deals with the mind; the mind controls the body, organs, voluntary and involuntary reflexes, muscles, nervous system, all areas of the brain, thoughts and feelings.

The Mind and Spirit are connected. Many practice prayer, meditation, and positive affirmations; these practices connect you to Source, God, Spirit, Universal mind, connecting your mind and spirit. The result of this connection is a feeling of fulfillment and contentment, a knowing, being spiritually aware. With prayer and meditation as a daily practice, you experience a pleasant fulfilling day and interact will those in your life in a positive way, attracting abundance and joy. Hypnosis accomplishes this altered state at an *even deeper level*. It creates a gateway to the mind and spirit, achieving a lasting desired change because you are *reprogramming* your subconscious mind.

The Spirit mind and body are connected; this is why if one of the three areas is out of balance, we say that there is *'dis-ease'*. Perfect balance is achieved with spirit + mind + body all in harmony. Hypnotherapy can help bring the body back in balance through direct communication with the mind, you control your own thoughts, reprogramming pain signals or limiting beliefs with new positive thoughts and beliefs.

"What is Hypnosis?" *Hypnosis is a natural state of selective heightened focused attention of the mind in which the mind relaxes in a state of trance to the point that conscious behavior* *stops.* The mind is relaxed in hypnosis, which is experienced as focused concentration, yet full awareness of self and surroundings remain, once the mind is relaxed in trance the conscious relaxes opening access to the subconscious mind where change takes place.

Elements of Hypnosis

Hypnosis has several elements which by themselves are not unique but when combined in hypnosis it allows for very effective and lasting change. The willingness to change must be present, in other words the emotional desire to change the behavior must be real. Emotions are a powerful tool when used for successful, effective change. Connecting emotions with hypnosis re-programming, using NLP (neuro linguistic programming) techniques with positive suggestions will help you *feel* like doing more of what you desire to do to succeed. We then add in the imagery and visualization (act as if, fake it until you make it) with emotions of desired change and this is a recipe for success.

Hyper-suggestibility, which is a heightened responsiveness to suggestion, instruction, and focused concentration, is another characteristic of hypnosis. A myth buster note here: An individual would never say or do anything that goes against their moral standards while in hypnosis. An example would be those on a stage, quacking like a duck, hopping on one foot, they had the emotional desire for their five minutes of fame. They were willing to act in a way that was acceptable to them, to achieve their desire of fame, attention and laughter. Hypnosis bypasses the filter in our mind that examines incoming ideas; this filter is what allows past beliefs from past experiences and interpretations to remain no matter how strong your 'will power' is to change them. It is important to relax the conscious mind, which will then allow the filter to open, facilitating the acceptance of new, positive, replacement programming in the subconscious mind. The replacement thoughts are supported through repetition in the form of trigger words or phrases and affirmations.

An extraordinary quality of mental, physical and emotional relaxation is an element of Hypnosis that many find amazing. This type of natural altered state of relaxation is not found in any other methods except perhaps in well practiced deep meditation. My clients have shared with me that for them, hypnosis is even more relaxing than meditation or a deep massage. Most clients experience a deep discharge of stress from all levels, from all areas of their mind and body. Being in hypnosis allows all of the systems in your body time to balance their functions, time to restore and re-energize, thirty minutes of hypnosis is similar to two hours of restful sleep.

Brain wave activity is an interesting element while in hypnosis, reflecting the deep relaxation the mind and body experiences. The brain wave levels are: Beta, this is your normal awake and alert state, Alpha relaxed, slightly altered state, you are able to access creative thinking, deep concentration, and possibly the level you are in when in prayer, Theta is the level for hypnosis and meditation, it is where you access memories, it is the state you are in as you fall asleep, and Delta is deep sleep, the level at which your body is relaxed enough to heal. Hypnosis accesses the Alpha, Theta and Delta levels of brain waves.

History of Hypnosis

Ritualistic ceremonies performed centuries ago are an example of an early form of hypnosis. A charismatic Leader or Holy Man, such as a High Priest, Shaman or Medicine Man, would lead their people in chanting or mantras, creating an altered state of concentrated focus, adding emotion to create an even more powerful ritual. An altered state during deep prayer and meditation is considered a form of hypnosis due to the change in brain wave activity.

Sigmund Freud was a supporter of hypnotherapy, and adopted _hypnotic regression_ as a therapeutic method. Freud can be credited with the application of psychoanalysis combined with hypnotic suggestion to hasten the outcome of successful treatment.

Emile Coue' developed a method used in hypnosis called _conscious autosuggestion._ He is credited with statement "Everyday and in every way I am getting better and better".

Edgar Cayce was known for his ability to go into a hypnotic trance and his ability as an _intuitive healer._ Cayce has also been referred to as a prophet, mystic and a seer.

"Can you imagine the many Applications for Hypnotherapy Today?"

- ❖ _Spiritual:_ reaching a quiet mind state without a struggle, connecting with your higher wisdom for guidance, fulfillment and purpose
- ❖ _Medical:_ accelerated recovery, chronic pain management, migraine relief, and cancer treatment side effects,

relaxation: to lower stress, blood pressure, pre and post surgery anxiety

❖ *Social:* smoking, weight loss, fears, phobias, financial success, improved quality relationships, career enhancement

❖ *Performance:* sports, accelerated learning

How do healing, pain reduction, improved learning skills, and relaxation occur with hypnosis? Access to the subconscious mind, reprogramming positive changes, affects the Autonomic Nervous System, changing the body response.

__Thoughts + Emotions = Behavior__

MIND creates imagination + thoughts = BODY creates reaction

Stress the body protects in a fear reaction

Relaxation allows the body to heal

__Anxiety = Fear = Pain__

Chronic pain loop

Anxiety creates fear, fear manifests pain, pain creates more anxiety and continues in a loop of anxiety creating fear, manifesting more pain, and more anxiety and on and on the thoughts continue causing the body to react in a constant state of heightened stress and pain. To reduce chronic pain we access the subconscious mind, reprogram the anticipation of the false pain signals, relaxing the body so it can restore itself back into balance.

We want to reprogram our subconscious from the fear mode that anticipates pain to a comfortable relaxed pain free state to eliminate or dial down the pain and discomfort. Chronic pain is different from acute pain. Acute pain is when the body is in protection mode, sending pain signals from the body only when necessary as a warning signal that something is wrong. Reducing acute pain can also be addressed with hypnosis; we affectively dial down the pain, not ignore it, but significantly lessen the pain to support the body in more efficient healing. Please consult your health care professional when you experience any type of pain. The information contained in this book is for self improvement purposes only. This is not a guide or substitute for professional medical treatment.

The hypnosis process employs the conscious mind to perform a redundant task, for example, staring at a spot above and concentrating on breathing. While the conscious mind is occupied, using visualization and imagination, to create a relaxed state, we bypass the filter between the conscious and subconscious mind, we access the sub conscious mind replacing undesired negative beliefs with positive new truths.

How does Hypnotherapy Work in Connecting to our Spirit?

As we learned earlier most of the beliefs and perceptions we have today were decided upon during the ages of two through seven, possibly pre birth and at a time during our life when we experience a trauma. These beliefs that no longer serve our highest good are stored in our subconscious mind, access to our subconscious is necessary to make successful lasting changes. With hypnosis we can change negative beliefs into positives, which change our thoughts, which change our emotions, which change how our physical body reacts resulting in complete Spirit Mind Body balance and harmony.

Hypnosis allows you to make contact with your Spirit; you true authentic self, connect with your true desires, ultimately your true passion, which is your Divine purpose. Buried long ago but not forgotten, the essence of you, your spirit is your true authentic self. Hypnosis supports us in our desire to eliminate the un-necessary baggage we carry through life, the emotional pain of loneliness and unworthiness. Reframe the false beliefs and the personal lies we decided about ourselves; by replacing our negative thoughts with *New* beliefs promoting higher self esteem, greater self love, and connect with higher self, our inner wisdom.

The practice of Self Hypnosis allows you immediate access to your subconscious mind to create positive lasting change through positive therapeutic suggestions. Listening to your self hypnosis recording in the first few weeks twice a day, then a minimum of once a day has been shown to be the most effective, repetition is very important for lasting change. Along with listening to self hypnosis recordings, positive affirmation cards, or 'post its', placed in private but frequently view spaces offer additional support in implementing positive change.

In Hypnosis, just as with the success of any new habit, we must practice with a commitment to the change we desire for effective and lasting success. As we mentioned earlier, much like prayer and meditation you have to want to make a change for the process to be effective. To pray without faith or sincerity or to meditate while thinking about a grocery list will not produce effective results. The same is true for hypnosis, if you are not willing or not responsive, self hypnosis will not be effective and a positive change will not occur. Responsiveness in hypnosis means demonstrating that your conscious mind is open and willing to accept input and the filter, or your mind's 'gate keeper', is open and receptive, allowing access to your subconscious mind, where positive changes take place.

The sub-conscious mind cannot distinguish between fact and fiction. This bears repeating to appreciate the power of this statement, imagine all the positive possibilities, *the sub-conscious mind cannot distinguish between fact and fiction!* In the process of replacing negative beliefs with the positive, we use the phrase 'more and more' to break down a new positive statement into believable portions.

The mind creates an image, thought or emotion; your body reacts. You do not have to physically perform a motion or action, just *think* about it and your body to reacts.

The subconscious mind does not distinguish fact from fiction.

Imagine a bright, shiny lemon, cut into it, see the juice dripping onto the plate, smell the fresh citrus aroma. Do you feel your salivary glands tingling? Do you have more saliva in your mouth?

Change your thoughts, Create your own reality, Control your health.

Self Hypnosis Exercises

Free Self Hypnosis Download on Website Code 'LOVE'

The following are practice exercises and examples of Self Hypnosis Scripts. I have included a script for relaxation and a script for chronic pain management. The self hypnosis exercise practice is about 30 minutes. These are available to download on my website at no charge. If you prefer your own voice, or more personal specific suggestions, perhaps an idea would be to record the following script into your computer, phone or recorder, and insert the appropriate positive suggestions to support the desired behavior or perception re-programming. Hypnosis is a unique experience for each one of us. My private session clients have described Hypnosis as though they are aware of everything around them, and during the first session wondering if they are even in hypnosis, this is because they feel fully aware, in control and able to comply with whatever is being asked *if they choose to do so.* Several of my clients compare hypnotherapy to a deep meditation that they enter into rapidly without the mind chatter or effort; some clients compare their session of 30 minutes to the relaxation of a two hour nap.

Hypnosis is very effective when you are receptive and have the strong desire to make a positive change in your quality of life.

Guided Relaxation Script for Self Hypnosis

Now I invite you to make yourself comfortable . . . *in whatever way possible . . . . in your chair, arms relaxed, feet flat on the floor . . . . or perhaps on the floor . . . sitting or lying down . . . . Your arms relaxed, legs uncrossed. And then if you would . . . . take in a nice gentle, deep breath . . . . in through your nose . . . filling up your lungs . . . . and as you exhale . . . and just **gently close your eyes down** . . . . Letting go of any concerns, any past or future thoughts or concerns . . . . Just relax into this moment.*

Keeping your eyes closed . . . Take in another nice deep breath . . . . breathing in peace and tranquility . . . . Breathe in through your nose . . . filling up your lungs so completely . . . . That your belly expands a bit . . . . Hold for a moment or two . . . . then a nice long gentle exhale . . . releasing any stress . . . any tension or anxiety held in your body . . .

Take in another nice deep breath . . . . breathing in . . . . filling up your lungs . . . hold for a moment or two . . . . then a long exhale . . . releasing any remaining stress . . . or tension . . . . held anywhere in your body . . . . and say to yourself the word . . . 'Relax'.

Again . . . . Take in a nice deep breath . . . . breathing in . . . . filling up your lungs . . . hold for a moment or two . . . . then a long exhale . . . . releasing any remaining stress or tension held anywhere in your body or in your mind . . . . And say to yourself the word 'relax'.

Now just breathe normally . . . a gentle . . . rhythmic breath . . . . in through your nose . . . . out through slightly parted lips . . . . Focusing on your breath . . . .

*Now as you relax . . . safe . . . comfortable . . . and at peace . . . . imagine sense . . . and feel . . . . a beautiful beam of white light . . . . coming down from above . . . . perhaps a Divine . . . healing light . . . and warm energy . . . . Of God . . . of Source . . . of Spirit . . . . descending down upon you from above . . . . to your crown chakra . . . . At the top of your head. Imagine . . . this beautiful white light of relaxing . . . healing . . . energy . . . flowing down from above . . . . Into the top of your head . . . . Relaxing energy . . . moving down through your forehead . . . . Releasing any tension in your brow . . . warm . . . . relaxing energy . . . . flowing down through your eyes . . . . Your eyelids . . . . smooth and relaxed . . . . relaxing healing energy . . . . moving down through your cheekbones . . . . down into your jaw muscles . . . your jaw muscles relaxed . . . . with slightly parted lips . . . . Send the beautiful . . . warm . . . relaxing . . . energy . . . down into your neck . . . . imagine . . . . all the neck muscles . . . . becoming loose and limp . . . . feel the warm . . . relaxing . . . energy . . . . moving down into your shoulders . . . . down into your arms . . . . Use the power of your imagination . . . . to send the warm . . . relaxing . . . healing . . . . Energy . . . down into your forearms . . . . down into your wrists . . . moving the healing energy down into your hands . . . . and all the way down . . . **can you imagine** . . . . Radiating . . . white light energy . . . out through your finger tips. **Breathe** . . .*

Imagine . . . sense . . . and feel the warm . . . relaxing . . . . Healing energy moving down now into your chest . . . . down through your back . . . . Warm . . . relaxing energy . . . Moving into all the back muscles . . . . the back muscles becoming loose . . . and limp . . . and relaxed. Send the warm . . . healing energy . . . . down into your hips and legs . . . . warm . . . relaxing . . . energy flows down into your knees and calves . . . . send the warm . . . relaxing . . . energy down into your ankles . . . . and feet . . . . relaxing energy flows all the way down into your feet . . . can you imagine white light energy . . . radiates out through your toes. **Breathe** *. . .*

This is the time when you might ask your Higher Self or your Inner Wisdom a question. For example "What is mine to do?" Or "Spirit please show me the solution now."

<u>Or</u>

Insert your positive therapeutic suggestions

<u>Sample Positive Suggestions</u>

More and more every day and in every way I feel self love growing inside of me

More and more every day and in every way I am more confident and courageous

Because fear is replaced by my courage, (Love, Faith), I have the strength to be aware of and feel my emotions

Every day in more ways I connect with Spirit, feel peace in thoughts of gratitude and love

Now *I am going to count from one to five and then you will return to the room fully aware. At the count of five your eyes are open, you are fully aware, feeling calm, rested, refreshed, and relaxed, remembering everything, looking forward to returning to hypnosis.*

One, *easily and gently you are returning to the room and your full awareness*

Two, your feel relaxed and refreshed

Three, you feel calm and rested

Four, you return remembering everything

Five, you are fully aware now, eyelids open, fully alert, back into the room, take in a gentle inhale and slowly exhale

<u>Imagery for Chronic Pain Management</u>

*Now I invite you to make yourself comfortable . . . in whatever way possible . . . . in your chair, arms relaxed, feet flat on the floor . . . . or perhaps on the floor . . . sitting or lying down . . . . Your arms relaxed, legs uncrossed. And then if you would . . . . take in a nice gentle, deep breath . . . . in through your nose . . . filling up your lungs . . . . and as you exhale . . . and just **gently close your eyes down** . . . . Letting go of any concerns, any past or future thoughts or concerns . . . . Just relax into this moment.*

Keeping your eyes closed . . . Take in another nice deep breath . . . . breathing in peace and tranquility . . . . Breathe in through your nose . . . filling up your lungs so completely . . . . That your belly expands a bit . . . . Hold for a moment or two . . . . then a nice long gentle exhale . . . releasing any stress . . . any tension or anxiety held in your body . . .

Take in another nice deep breath . . . . breathing in . . . . filling up your lungs . . . hold for a moment or two . . . . then a long exhale . . . releasing any remaining stress . . . or tension . . . . held anywhere in your body . . . . and say to yourself the word . . . 'Relax'.

Again . . . . Take in a nice deep breath . . . . breathing in peace . . . . filling up your lungs . . . hold for a moment or two . . . . then a long exhale . . . . releasing any remaining stress or tension held anywhere in your body or in your mind . . . . And say to yourself the word 'relax'.

Now just breathe normally . . . a gentle . . . rhythmic breath . . . .
in through your nose . . . . out through slightly parted lips . . . .
Focusing on your breath . . . .

Now as you relax . . . safe . . . comfortable . . . and at peace . . . .
imagine sense . . . and feel . . . . a beautiful beam of white
light . . . . coming down from above . . . . perhaps a Divine . . .
healing light . . . and warm energy . . . . Of God . . . of Source . . .
of Spirit . . . . descending down upon you from above . . . . to
your crown chakra . . . . At the top of your head. Imagine . . . this
beautiful white light of relaxing . . . healing . . . energy . . . flowing
down from above . . . . Into the top of your head . . . . Relaxing
energy . . . moving down through your forehead . . . . Releasing
any tension in your brow . . . warm . . . . relaxing energy . . . .
flowing down through your eyes . . . . Your eyelids . . . . smooth
and relaxed . . . . relaxing healing energy . . . . moving down
through your cheekbones . . . . down into your jaw muscles . . .
your jaw muscles relaxed . . . . with slightly parted lips . . . .
Send the beautiful . . . warm . . . relaxing . . . energy . . . down
into your neck . . . . imagine . . . . all the neck muscles . . . .
becoming loose and limp . . . . feel the warm . . . relaxing . . .
energy . . . . moving down into your shoulders . . . . down into
your arms . . . . Use the power of your imagination . . . . to send
the warm . . . relaxing . . . healing . . . . Energy . . . down into
your forearms . . . . down into your wrists . . . moving the healing
energy down into your hands . . . . and all the way down . . .
can you imagine *. . . . Radiating . . . white light energy . . . out*
through your finger tips. **Breathe** *. . .*

Imagine . . . sense . . . and feel the warm . . . relaxing . . . . Healing
energy moving down now into your chest . . . . down through

your back . . . . Warm . . . relaxing energy . . . Moving into all the back muscles . . . . the back muscles becoming loose . . . and limp . . . and relaxed. Send the warm . . . healing energy . . . . down into your hips and legs . . . . warm . . . relaxing . . . energy flows down into your knees and calves . . . . send the warm . . . relaxing . . . energy down into your ankles . . . . and feet . . . . relaxing energy flows all the way down into your feet . . . can you imagine white light energy . . . radiates out through your toes. **Breathe** *. . .*

Imagine that you are floating in a way in which you feel safe and comfortable, floating on a cloud . . . or a gently flowing river. Feel deeper and more relaxed with every breath. Each time you exhale . . . you let a little more tension out of your body. While you remain in this pleasant state of safe . . . comfortable floating relaxation . . . notice how your body is feeling. As you float along . . . be aware of your body and all of its sensations.

Imagine sense and feel a beautiful white . . . healing light . . . glowing all around you. Imagine this beautiful light radiating healing energy through every cell . . . every organ . . . every bone . . . radiating healing energy through all the tissue and skin . . . . sending a healing light all through your body . . . Imagine this radiating healing energy begins at the top of your head, down to your forehead, down to your face, your neck, healing energy down to your shoulders, your arms, down to your hands and out through your fingers. Imagine sense and feel the healing white light filling up your chest and back, traveling down your hips and thighs, healing energy down into your knees, your calf, your ankles, and out through your toes.

Now as you breathe in . . . feel the relaxing comfort of the healing white light all through your body. As you exhale . . . you exhale any pain or discomfort or tension . . . release it completely . . . sending healing energy where necessary in your body. Your entire body bathed in this healing white light. You feel the healing glow all through your body . . . feeling comfort . . . relaxation . . . imagine, sense and feel healing in progress . . . the beautiful white glow radiating all through in and around your body. Breathe in the healing relaxation and comfort.

Now gently scan your body from the top of your head to the tips of your toes. Just notice if a particular location or part of your body is asking for additional healing white light. Just spend as much time as you need in that area to allow your body to do its perfect work for you. As you rest while your body restores itself.

Perhaps you imagine healing angels with magic fingers loosening any discomfort in a particular area of your body, or can you imagine a dial with numbers, 10 highest discomfort level down to 1, relaxing comfort. I wonder if you could feel your pain or discomfort, could you possibly give it a number? Now imagine as you dial down any discomfort, watch the dial, perhaps digital numbers, go down into complete relaxation, 7, 6, 5, 4, 3, 2, 1 comfort,

Feel the healing white light relaxing and loosening the muscles and tendons, supporting healthy blood flow, renewing healthy cells, oxygenating the blood, healthy blood pumping though the healthy organs. Can you imagine any discomfort dissolving up into the atmosphere as you focus on this pleasant sense of safety and comfort, perhaps floating on the clouds? Imagine comfort and relaxation all through your body as the healing white light completes its perfect job for you.

Rest here for a moment feel your body doing its perfect healing work for you. Enjoy being at peace, floating, comfortable, and safe.

Sample Positive Suggestions for Health

More and More every day, with each breath, I relax more and more, releasing healing energy all through my body

If pain alerts me to a need for healing, with love I send healing light to renew and restore my body.

Every day and in every way I am getting healthier and healthier.

Because my body is doing its perfect work, my cells are healthy and strong, my organs are renewed and healthy

More and more everyday with every breath my body sends healthy energy to repair, renew and restore comfort and health where my body needs it most.

Now I am going to count from one to five and then you will return to the room fully aware. At the count of five your eyes are open, you are fully aware, feeling calm, rested, refreshed, and relaxed, remembering everything, looking forward to returning to hypnosis.

One, easily, and gently you are returning to the room and your full awareness

Two, your feel relaxed and refreshed

Three, you feel calm and rested

Four, you return remembering everything

Five, you are fully aware now, eyelids open, fully alert, back into the room, take in a gentle inhale and slowly exhale

Creating Positive Affirmations and Therapeutic Suggestions

Therapeutic suggestions used in self hypnosis and positive affirmations are often the same. Positive Affirmations and therapeutic suggestions are a wonderful, valuable daily practices when combined with self hypnosis, prayer or meditation.

Repetition is the key to successfully accomplishing lasting change. Write your affirmations on cards or 'post its' and place them in private areas so you will see them and read them throughout the day. Read them as many times as possible to support your desired changes. Create a variety of affirmations and suggestions; shuffle them to keep them fresh and meaningful. Write new ones whenever you feel the need. Always make the statement in the positive, using the present tense. If the affirmation or suggestion is not yet 'believable' to you, break the desired new belief down into a more believable statement by the use of the phrase, *'more and more every day and in every way'*, or *'every day in more ways'*.

More and more every day and in every way . . . .

1.

2.

3.

Every day in more ways . . .

1.

2.

3.

Because . . . .

1.

2.

3.

Reminder Please Note: *Hypnotherapy is not a medical treatment or a substitute for medical treatment.* Hypnotherapy, hypnosis and self hypnosis are used for self improvement and learning purposes only. If you have a health issue please contact your health care professional.

Sample Positive Therapeutic Suggestions and Affirmations

More and more every day and in every way . . . .

I feel self love growing inside of me

I am more confident and courageous

Fear is replaced by my courage, (Love, Faith)

I have the courage to feel my emotions

I have the courage and strength to be aware of and feel my emotions

I am stronger and more in control of my life

Decisions come more easily for me

I feel energized, I enjoy healthy exercise to clear my mind and I feel my happiness increase

I am a beautiful child of the universe, Loved and supported, connected to higher source.

I connect with inner peace as I fill my mind with thoughts of gratitude and love

My self–awareness is growing

My intuition, my connection to my higher wisdom, is growing stronger and stronger

I quiet my mind, opening the channels for greater connection to source

I am filled with strength, confidence and the power to fulfill my perfect self expression

All of my energies come together to support me in achieving my highest potential

I am aware that all I need is available to me whenever I need it

I remain calm and relaxed by taking 3 deep breaths breathing in peace and exhale any tension or stress to relax and re center myself through the day

Because I take time to quiet my mind, I connect with my Spirit, I connect with my inner child, more and more I connect with my creative side

Because I pay more attention to how I feel, I am more aware of what makes me happy, more and more I take time to enjoy every day

Because I choose how I feel, I choose to be happy

Because I choose to be Happy, I look forward to each morning with renewed energy; I look forward to each day with passion.

Health

More and more every day and in every way . . . .

I am grateful to be alive

I am worthy to live and enjoy a full healthy life

I visualize each cell of my body radiating wholeness

My healthy cells easily repair any damage the medical treatment might do

I have an army of white blood cells that is vast powerful and easily overwhelms any and all cancer cells

My white blood cells are aggressive, eager and quick to seek out and destroy any and all cancer cells

I am whole and well in spirit mind and body

I open my mind and heart to divine healing.

I give thanks for those who have the skills, knowledge and wisdom to help me heal and I allow them to do so.

I see myself as perfect, healthy and strong.

More and more I feel abundant health as the truth for me

I feel self love growing inside of me

I support my health more and more by consuming healthy Nutritious fresh foods to Fuel my Body

Because I imagine and feel the cancer cells weak and confused.
The dead cancer cells are easily flushed out of the body

Because my body grows healthier and stronger more and more
I am confident, relaxed and comfortable

Because I value my health, I take time throughout my day to relax
with 3 deep breaths, re-centering and renewing my energy

Because I appreciate myself, more and more I take the positive
actions necessary to support my perfect health.

Spiritual

More and More every day . . . .

With a cleansing breath, I re-center in God's peace that is always available to me

With joy, I give thanks for all of the blessings in my life.

I welcome new opportunities to be a channel for God's flow of abundant good

Empowered by faith I am confident and courageous

I relax in confidence that I am loved and supported by God and those who love me.

More and more as I grow stronger in my health and faith I rest in the comfort of God's love and protection.

More and more I feel the presence of God in me.

I am loved, connected and supported by God.

Every day is an opportunity to heal and grow emotionally, physically and spiritually

I am strengthened as I focus on my oneness with God

Additional Reading Suggestions

Bernard, Joseph M., PhD, *"Awaken"*

Butterworth, Eric, *"Discover the Power Within You"*

Chopra, Deepak

"Spiritual Solutions"

"The Ultimate Happiness Prescription"

Sonia Choquette,

"Grace, Guidance and Gifts"

"Heart's Desire"

"The Power of Your Spirit"

"Soul Lessons"

Dyer, Wayne, Dr., *"Wishes Fulfilled"*

Goddard, Nevelle, *"The Power of Awareness Letting Go"*

Hawkins, David, MD, PhD, *"The Pathway to Surrender"*

Hay, Louise, *"You Can Heal your Life"*

Hay, Louise & Richardson, Cheryl, *"How to Create an Exceptional Life"*

Hicks, Esther & Jerry, *"Ask and It is Given"*

Holmes, Ernest, *"This Thing Called You"*

Jampolsky, Gerald G., MD, *"Love is Letting Go of Fear"*

Katie, Byron, *"Loving What Is"*

Blackburn Losey, Meg, PhD, *"The Art of Living Out Loud"*

Myss, Caroline, *"Invisible Acts of Power"*

Oswald, Yvonne, *"Every Word Has Power"*

Peters, Ronald L., MD, MPH,

"Edgework, Exploring the Psychology of Disease"

Singer, Michael A., *"The Untethered Soul"*

Tolle, Eckhart, *"Living in the Now"*

Truman, Karol K., *"Feelings Buried Alive Never Die"*

Williamson, Marianne

"Law of Divine Compensation"

"Return to Love"

Zukav, Gary, *"The Heart of the Soul"*

"An introduction to A Course in Miracles", Miracle Distribution Center

"Daily Word", Unity

"40 Days of Thankful Living", Unity of Phoenix

"The New Game of Life and How to Play It", original text by Florence Scovel Shinn, *edited by Ruth L. Miller*

ALL THAT I AM

I AM GRATEFUL FOR ALL THAT I AM,
ALL THAT I SEE, ALL THAT I LOVE,
ALL THAT HAS BEEN GIVEN TO ME

I AM WILLING TO ACCEPT MY GIFTS,
FROM A PLACE OF LOVE, SERVING
MY DIVINE PURPOSE

I AM AT PEACE, I AM JOYFUL
I AM CONNECTED, I AM LOVED

I AM LIVING MY LIGHT,
THE SPIRIT IN ME IS ALL THAT I AM

by Susan Faye Davis

Additional Teachings & Services by the Author

Susan Faye Davis currently resides in Scottsdale, Arizona were she is passionately involved, as creator and president, of *"Changes from the Inside Out Weight Management Program"*. *Changes* is a unique program specifically designed to address healthy weight management from the inside out; we focus on the *'you'* inside. We examine the current limiting beliefs and thoughts that have prevented successful and lasting, healthy weight management. Together with your desire and our methods we change and reprogram your limiting beliefs into positive supportive beliefs and behaviors for successful and lasting healthy weight management. This dynamic program, unlike any other, combines the successful application of safe and natural techniques to achieve healthy balance of your Spirit Mind and Body. This comprehensive program supports you in your desire to change into the *'you'* you are ready to become. *Healthy thoughts on the inside result in healthy appearances on the outside.* www.changesweightmanagement.com

Susan is a certified medical support clinical hypnotherapist, master herbalist, nutritional consultant and a holistic health practitioner. She offers private sessions, workshops and self hypnosis CDs through her private practice, www.susandavishypnotherapy.com.

Susan currently serves on the Unity of Phoenix Board of Trustees, an alumnus of the Hypnotherapy Academy of America, NM, is a member of the International Board of Hypnotherapy and the Arizona Holistic Chamber of Commerce.

Free meditation and self hypnosis downloads are available on this website: www.susanfayedavis.com